PROFESSOR BERMAN

PROFESSOR BERMAN

The Last Lecture of Minnesota's Greatest Public Historian

HY BERMAN
with Jay Weiner

University of Minnesota Press
Minneapolis
London

All photographs appear courtesy of the Berman family unless credited otherwise.

Published by the University of Minnesota Press
111 Third Avenue South, Suite 290
Minneapolis, MN 55401-2520
http://www.upress.umn.edu

Printed in the United States of America on acid-free paper

The University of Minnesota is an equal-opportunity educator and employer.

25 24 23 22 21 20 19   10 9 8 7 6 5 4 3 2 1

Library of Congress Cataloging-in-Publication Data
Names: Berman, Hyman, 1925–2015, author. | Weiner, Jay, author.
Title: Professor Berman : the last lecture of Minnesota's greatest public historian / Hy Berman with Jay Weiner.
Description: Minneapolis : University of Minnesota Press, [2019] | Includes bibliographical references and index. |
Identifiers: LCCN 2019001519 (print) | ISBN 978-1-5179-0106-6 (hc/j)
Subjects: LCSH: Berman, Hyman, 1925-2015. | Public historians—United States—Biography. | College teachers—Minnesota—Biography. | Minneapolis (Minn.)—Biography.
Classification: LCC E175.5.B47 A3 2019 (print) | DDC 973.07202 [B] —dc23
LC record available at https://lccn.loc.gov/2019001519

For Betty

I always saw the public arena as a massive classroom.

—*Hy Berman*

CONTENTS

FOREWORD
How It All Happened

Jay Weiner

My greatest accomplishment so far is the sum total of everything ... not any one thing, not any one book, not any one article, but the sum total of it all.
—Hy Berman

On a good, old-fashioned clear and chilly December Thursday in 2015, in a plain pine casket with a Star of David carved atop it, Professor Hyman Berman, Minnesota's most noted public historian and one of the University of Minnesota's most beloved teachers, was laid to rest. He was nearly ninety-one years old and, until months before, was as vibrant, sharp, and charming as ever. His unexpected and rapid decline had begun on July 29, 2015, when he attended a Minnesota Twins baseball game with his younger brother, Harold. "And the damn Twins lost, too," Hy said.

Soon after he fell ill, his kidneys began to fail, and I saw him on October 27, 2015, for the final time. The first round of interviews for this book project was complete, and we both felt really good about how our months of conversations had gone. The outline was done and the first chapter's draft under way. On this autumn day, he sat for a photo shoot with photographer Terry Gydesen at his home and he looked terrific. The dialysis seemed to be working. His healthy skin color was back. He'd abandoned the cane he had used after a fall about eighteen months earlier. He took off his glasses, and the photograph on this book's back flap shows a distinguished, proud, and fully engaged Hy Berman.

In my role then as speechwriter to University of Minnesota president Eric Kaler, I soon after traveled to Hong Kong and Seoul with plans to begin writing Hy's memoirs with him upon my return and to conduct follow-up interviews to fill the holes we knew existed. I was to start, he was to edit, and we were to complete this in time for him to bask in it.

A few days after my return from Asia, we spoke by phone. It was the Tuesday before Thanksgiving 2015, and he said, "I'm not doing very well." His blood pressure was low. His white blood count was down, along, uncharacteristically, I could tell through the phone, with his spirits. We set a lunch date for the following Tuesday, December 1.

It never happened. Hy Berman died at his home just off West River Parkway in Minneapolis on Sunday, November 29, 2015.

For nearly thirty years, I was a reporter for the Minneapolis-based *Star Tribune,* and a search of my clippings reveals that I never quoted Hy Berman. And although he was the all-time most frequent guest on Twin Cities Public Television's *Almanac* public affairs program and I was an occasional analyst, our paths never crossed there.

But over the years, Hy's friend and pharmacist—and my friend and pharmacist—Tom SenGupta brought us together. Tom was the long-time owner of Schneider Drug on University Avenue in Minneapolis's Prospect Park neighborhood, a store known for its colorful murals and posters supporting Paul Wellstone, single-payer health care, and investments in public education. For decades, Tom hosted occasional week-night salons with political candidates, authors, and activists as a gaggle of about thirty (mostly retired professors, aging hippies, and community gadflies) gathered around a potbelly stove in the middle of his pharmacy. I'm sure it was there that I first heard Hy and his passion for working people, his remarkable interpretations of history, and his humor.

About a decade ago, I got to know him a bit better. Hy and Tom began collaborating on an idea to create a monument or a gathering spot or an organization to honor "the common man." It was an amorphous but bold vision, and they struggled to nail down a concept, a location, and funding. Along with local sculptor Doug Freeman, they began meeting for dinner five or six times a year at Caffe Biaggio on St. Paul's University Avenue, and they invited others to join them and brainstorm. Tom invited me, and I became a regular participant, drinking martinis, eating pasta, and sharing stories with Hy. He told many of the same tales just about every dinner, a sort of greatest hits from a rock star. The stories never got old.

In February 2015 I was delighted to receive an invitation to Hy's ninetieth birthday, which he celebrated with his friend and fellow nonagenarian David Noble, the professor who recruited him to the University in 1961. There, in Noble's living room, removed from the noise and hoopla, Hy and I chatted, and I asked if anyone had ever sat him down and recorded his stories.

"No," he said dismissively and, I would soon learn, inaccurately. "Nobody wants to hear my stories."

I told him someone should at least get his Mark Dayton and Rudy Perpich and Hubert Humphrey stories on tape for posterity. He shrugged, accepted the idea, acquiesced, and a few weeks later I visited Hy at his home with no agenda, goal, or motive other than to get an hour or two of anecdotes on my digital recorder. I had no idea what I would do with the stories.

We sat in his living room, which was lined with hundreds of books and adorned with spectacular paintings and sculpture by some of Minnesota's greatest artists, such as George Morrison and Cameron Booth. Hy showed me a thick, blue, three-ring binder. He explained it contained the transcripts of interviews (he *had* recorded many of his stories!) and some rough chapters he had worked on eight years earlier with California State University, Long Beach political scientist Jack Stuart. The idea was to transform those interviews into a book of Hy's memoirs, but the two could never get their act together even though the University of Minnesota Press wanted Hy's memoirs and Hy wanted to make them happen. He had asked other potential collaborators in town to assist but no one bit, and he needed help to complete this book project.

As he handed the binder to me, our eyes met and he said, "What do you think?"

I'd never been hypnotized before, but, when a man of Hy Berman's stature, magnetism, and cuteness stares at you and suggests he'd like you as a partner, it's kind of tough to resist.

"Sure, I'd love to help," I said instantly, without understanding what I'd gotten myself into. What a wonderful spur-of-the-moment decision I'd made and privilege I'd stumbled on.

Thus began, over a seven-month period, a sporadic dozen sessions of about two hours each at his home, mostly at the end of my Friday workdays. I developed my questions around the Stuart interviews and aimed to fill in missing gaps in them. I also dived more deeply into Hy's relationships with key historic figures. We obtained his FBI files via the Freedom of Information Act, and what we found answered some questions for him. He directed me to some of his earliest writings, and I tracked down the House Un-American Activities Committee testimony in which Hy was mentioned, as well as some of his newspaper commentaries. It was truly fun.

On several occasions I sat beside him and watched his *Almanac* TV appearances and other lengthy videotaped interviews, reviewing what he had said and confirming that using that material was okay with him. "I'd say the same thing today," he said. All told, I gathered perhaps thirty-five to forty hours of Hy Berman sound.

Hy and I developed the outline for this book together. He approved updates to it after a meeting with University of Minnesota Press editor Erik Anderson. The three of us conducted that final meeting in his hospital room. Hy also read and liked the beginning sections of the first chapter I shared with him. Sadly, that's all he saw.

During our first full interview session, Hy and I quickly agreed on the direction and tone of the book: that it would be Hy Berman talking directly to Minnesotans, historians, and lovers of political storytelling. My job was to organize his words, serving as a conduit to bring his unmistakable voice and his extraordinary life to print. This was designed to be a Hy Berman lecture about himself.

During one of our first full-blown interview sessions in the spring of 2015, I said to him enthusiastically and ambitiously, "I think we can get this done pretty quickly."

He responded, "We'd better."

Fewer than nine months later, Hy was gone.

A major portion of his words and wisdom here comes from the interviews conducted in 2007 by political scientist Jack Stuart. Hy was, and I am, grateful to Jack for sharing those transcripts and early draft chapters with us.

Additional material resulted from the interviews I conducted with Hy.

Other words and stories come from assorted interviews—especially a lengthy one in 1984 with University of Minnesota colleague Clarke A. Chambers. I used words from some of Hy's appearances on *Almanac,* and from other recorded lectures and radio and TV interviews. In some cases I merged segments of different interviews that addressed similar topics or themes. As best I could, if these words did not come from *Almanac,* the Stuart or Chambers interviews, or my interviews with Hy, I have identified the source.

I edited and tweaked for grammar and clarity. I used some poetic license to write transitional sentences. Hy knew I was going to do this. That was the role he wanted me to play. In the end, about 95 percent of the words here are untouched, written as Hy spoke them (or, in some cases, as he wrote them).

In many ways, Hy's life was a series of dramatic transitions: Eastern European immigrants' son to Minnesota expert; Communist true believer to "traitorous" outcast and New Deal liberal; aspiring New York academic to down-to-earth midwestern public TV personality.

No matter what stage of his life or what public stage he stole, he was always in the middle of things, and he loved that. As much as possible, as best as I could, this book is how Hy wanted his story told.

1 Growing Up Comrade

Culture shock hit me instantly when I landed at Wold-Chamberlain Field, the Minneapolis–St. Paul airport. It was the early winter of 1961.

I had come from New York where the airports were full of black and brown people doing the menial work. Detroit, where I was coming from that day from my job at Michigan State University, was also filled with people of color doing the dirty work in public facilities. I was an up-and-coming U.S. labor historian, but you didn't need a Ph.D. to know that the grunt work in this country in the 1960s was performed by African Americans and Latino Americans.

Then I arrived in Minnesota to give a lecture at the University of Minnesota about the Great Railroad Strike of 1877, one of the nation's first workers' uprisings. I walked through the airport to get my luggage, and I was shocked to see that all the people with the brooms, all the people emptying the trash, and all the people cleaning the bathrooms had blond hair and blue eyes. What the hell had happened to the world? It was topsy-turvy. And I said to myself, "Well, this sure is an interesting place."

That was my first impression of Minnesota—that it was different from anything I'd seen before or anyplace I'd been before. At thirty-six years old, I felt like a short Jewish stranger in a strange Scandinavian, Gentile land. Soon, when I got to the University of Minnesota campus, I noticed, too, how different the faculty was from my experiences at New York's City College, where I had been an undergraduate, and Columbia University, where I received my Ph.D. I mean, where were all the Jews?

Whatever world it was, I'd entered it quickly and unexpectedly. My wife, Betty, and I had moved only months earlier from New York to East Lansing, Michigan. I had just established my new and even long-awaited academic trajectory at a respected Big Ten university, Michigan State. But a lecture on the University of Minnesota campus and an instant offer compelled me to make a sudden move to this seemingly foreign place.

Little did I know that for the next half century this different place would become my family's home and my academic home base. Little did I know that I would become Minnesota's unofficial "people's historian," translating the state's history and politics, while making a little bit of history of my own.

If my arrival in Minnesota was filled with surprises, imagine what it was like for my parents when they arrived in the United States by way of Canada almost fifty years earlier. Talk about entering a strange and foreign place, and imagine the profound transitions that one faces in his or her life.

I was born in the United States, but my parents were not. So I lived a true immigrant's life in New York, with Yiddish as my first language. That first immigration in my DNA began in 1913, when my father, David, fled Lodz, Poland, for America. Eight years later, my mother, Yetta Braun, arrived. My life as the son of Jewish left-wing immigrant garment workers and small business owners molded who I became, what I believed, and the path of my eventual scholarship.

They left repression behind, but not their politics. In a sense, my parents paved my way to Minnesota, to this once-strange land. In just about every way, they made me who I am today.

My First Word Was "Bolshevik"

On February 20, 1925, I was born into an immigrant milieu.

We lived on Surf Avenue, the main thoroughfare running through Coney Island, Brooklyn, New York. Coney Island was, and continues to be, a summer haven for poor and immigrant families seeking to escape the heat of the city. The attractions of the seashore were accompanied by popular entertainment for the masses, and the result was a noisy environment of fun, with crowds enjoying roller coasters, popular music in inexpensive restaurants, and games of chance. It was into this scene of freak shows, hot dog stands, and amusement parks that I was born and developed.

My father left Poland at the age of sixteen because he was part of a militant self-defense youth organization that retaliated against attacks on Jews. When I was about ten or eleven years old, my father admitted something to me. Yes, he said, he actually killed an anti-Semitic Pole in Lodz. That's why he came to the United States. He had to. He was on the run. So you can see the depth of his political passions.

He was already in the militant wing of the Bund, which was the major organization of Jewish workers and Socialists in Russia, Poland, and Lithuania. Consequently, when he came to the United States and started working in the garment industry, he was immediately attracted to its left-wing forces.

In 1919, when the U.S. Socialist Party split, he was in the group that rebelled against what he considered to be the party's lack of revolutionary militancy, and went into what later became the Communist Party. He was in the Jewish Federation of the Socialist Party, which was essentially the Bund in the United States, and during the ideological splits that took place after the First World War, he, again, naturally was in the furthest of the left wing.

My mother came to the United States also from Poland after World War I. If anything, she was more militant than my father. She considered my father's trade union compromises as being unforgivable. But were they compromises? I don't think so.

My father was a sewing machine operator working primarily in factories, producing men's and boys' garments. He also was one of the founders of the Amalgamated Clothing Workers Union of America. In the year I was born, 1925, a major factional, ideological conflict was taking place in the garment unions that led to a massive internal war within the International Ladies Garment Workers Union, or ILGWU, and a minor struggle of the same kind in the men's Amalgamated Clothing Workers Union. That's where he split with Sidney Hillman, the founding president of the ACWU, on questions of internal union politics. The split between Hillman and my father's group was such that it led to my father's being able to get only part-time work before being blacklisted and expelled from the union. Let's just say David Berman wasn't a big fan of Sidney Hillman, and vice versa.

My father's commitment to union democracy had an impact on many others, including on at least one man I met, believe it or not, decades later when I was in China. This episode reminds me how close-knit the world is and how universal politics can get. In 1983 I was lecturing in Beijing at the Chinese Association for International Understanding to a group that included some old Chinese revolutionaries. After my lecture, an old man in his eighties came over to me and said that he was in the United States in the early 1930s. He was, in fact, working in New York in the garment industry.

He was sent by the Chinese Communist Party to be its liaison in the United States and he was a staffer in an office that was called something like the Committee for Chinese Democracy. But he had to earn a living because they weren't able to pay him.

So, he went to work for Sidney Hillman in the ACWU as a kind of organizer for the Chinese sweatshop workers in New York's Chinatown. This Chinese man said to me, "Do you think I was grateful to Mr. Hillman? No. I joined the left-wing opposition to him." I said, "It's understandable." Then, we started talking some more.

I said, "You may have known my father."

He looked at me and he turned pale. "You're not Dave's son, are you?"

There, in the middle of Beijing, he told me I had bounced on his knee a half century earlier. With that, the attitude toward me changed overnight after he reported to the Chinese officials who I was and who my father was. From then on, when I was introduced for my lectures in China, I was no longer Professor Berman. I was "Comrade Berman." Whoa, I thought. I had to make it very clear. "My *father* was Comrade Berman. I'm Professor Berman."

Making a living and starting a family while working irregularly was impossible for my father, so he opened a soda stand on Coney Island. He then took on the role of a worker and small-business man who lived on the edge of poverty. I understood later on as a historian that this was a very common phenomenon of the Jewish immigrant experience.

My first contact with the Communist Party, according to my parents, was that the first word out of my mouth was "Bolshevik." I kind of doubt that, but that's what they told me. This, of course, gives you an indication of my family background and their aspirations for me.

My parents also told me that at the age of two or three, I was taken to rallies at Madison Square Garden and at Union Square, and to May Day parades. They told me my first May Day parade was at the age of one. That would have been 1926, or forty years after the first May Day, which was staged—most people don't know—for *American* workers to gain the eight-hour workday. I wish we'd celebrate it again. It's viewed as a Communist holiday, but it has its roots here in the United States and we should reclaim it. But I'm not holding my breath for that.

My earliest recollection of political activity that I directly engaged in was when I was in elementary school in Public School 23 in the Bronx, where we'd moved. There was a hunger demonstration or march staged by the Communist Party. I was then in second grade, and I got up in class and demanded that my classmates walk out with me to the demonstration. My teacher thought I was crazy and didn't know what I was talking about. When I said we wanted an unemployment insurance bill passed in Congress, he said, "In second grade we don't talk about these things."

For that outburst, I got into trouble. The irony was that the trouble was reported to my parents, who separated the political content from the fact that I got in trouble in school. They punished me because I shouldn't get in trouble in school, even if it was for political reasons.

Another phenomenon of the immigrant experience was the constant moving, either because of job changes or because of the difficulty of keeping up with rent payments. Voluntary moves also were made to take advantage of rent concessions made by distressed landlords seeking to attract tenants. Landlords, who were looking to rent vacant apartments, would offer deals—two or three months' free rent to anyone willing to stay for at least three months. Many immigrant families on the edge of poverty would often move twice a year, three months' free rent and then three months of paying rent. So we moved quite frequently, from Coney Island to Flatbush, to Crown Heights—all in Brooklyn—and then to the South Bronx.

The South Bronx was a densely settled community of predominantly Eastern European Jewish immigrants. A significant minority of Italian working-class and Irish immigrants lived in pockets of blocks within the South Bronx. For many years as I grew up, I thought there were only two types of people in the world: Jews and Catholics. I never heard of Protestants. Protestants didn't exist. When I discovered later on in school that Protestants were the majority in this country I couldn't believe it because I had never seen one.

My father's blacklisting from his union coincided with the onset of the Great Depression. By 1930, when both my father and mother were jobless, and I was five years old and my brother, Harold, was two years old, we found ourselves destitute living on Intervale Avenue and 165th Street.

My uncle and aunt, my mother's sister and her husband, had a small grocery store a block away. Either you were an immigrant worker in the garment trades or you were a small retail merchant selling commodities to the poor garment workers who didn't have jobs to pay for what they bought. It was a kind of vicious circle, but the retail merchants were a little bit better off than the garment workers.

Despite the Depression, a whole new block of stores was built on 165th Street. My uncle moved out of his grocery store around the corner on Rogers Place into one in the new block of stores. The landlord of the grocery store from which he had moved retaliated by opening a new, competing grocery store in the one my uncle vacated. Next to the landlord's newly opened grocery store was a candy store long owned by the landlord. So my uncle, in retaliation, opened a competing candy store and put my father in it. These were combative people.

My father was jobless and was delighted to have an opportunity to run a candy store, which was an early version of a convenience store, with tobacco, newspapers, snacks, and, of course, candy. Fortunately, my father had a more outgoing personality than the competing candy store landlord around the corner. My uncle and aunt were nicer people than that landlord and small grocery owner, so they beat him out too. Within two years, both stores around the corner went out of business and my uncle's and my father's stores became the only grocery and candy stores in the neighborhood.

Diagonally across Intervale Avenue was the Minsker Shul, the orthodox synagogue established by people from Minsk in what was then Byelorussia. But, actually, not everybody in the neighborhood was from Minsk. In fact, very few were from Minsk. They were from all parts of the former Pale, where Jews were allowed to live—Russia, Poland, Ukraine, and Byelorussia, as well as the Romanian and Austro-Hungarian regions.

The people I knew didn't go to the Minsker Shul. The people I knew marched up and down in front of the Minsker Shul on Yom Kippur with ham sandwiches to demonstrate pretty clearly that they were not only secular but also staunchly antireligious and independent of the superstition of religiosity. As usual, those Jews couldn't agree on anything.

That put my father in a difficult position. His radical proclivities were limited in that, being a storekeeper, he had to be a friend to all people. He had to keep his political sentiments to himself, except that on the newsstand he prominently featured the Communist newspapers—*Freiheit* and *Daily Worker*—and put the *Daily News, Mirror, Journal,* and, of course, the *Wall Street Journal* in subordinate positions. The *New York Times* did have a place of honor on the newsstand right next to the *Daily Worker.* That was some kind of political hierarchy there.

That didn't prevent him from speaking out when need occurred, once even closing the store on May first, or May Day, which he considered International Workers' Day. You should know, a candy store never closes in New York. How else can people buy a newspaper or a cigar? It's always open, except for Rosh Hashanah and Yom Kippur, the Jewish High Holidays.

If my father were true to his ideological position, he would have closed the store on May Day every year and kept it open on Rosh Hashanah and Yom Kippur. But he had to compromise. The one time he closed it on May Day it caused a big fuss, not with the *Forward* readers, who were Social Democrats but still socialists and atheists, but with Minsker Shul attendees, who, if there had been another candy store in the neighborhood, would have probably walked out of our candy store to the other candy store and gotten their two cents plain there instead of at our store.

Two cents plain, for those of you who are not familiar with it, was plain soda water. For two cents you got a big glass of soda water. If you wanted some syrup in the soda water, it cost you another three cents, or a whole nickel. But two cents plain is what most people could afford. They would have bought their two cents plain at a competitor, but we had no competitor, so it was an absolute necessity that they come into the store.

Ultimately, my father learned his lesson. On May Day, he sent me off to the demonstrations, or he put my mother behind the counter and he went, or my mother went and he was behind the counter, but the store was always open. But on Rosh Hashanah and Yom Kippur it was always closed. Those are the painful compromises a retail merchant has to make as a radical atheist entrepreneur serving a predominantly religious immigrant community.

My first schooling, even before I went to the Yiddish shul—or what you'd call Hebrew school today—was at PS 23. I was five years old and in kindergarten. The first day of school was traumatic for me in many ways. I remember being completely enveloped in fear, uncertainty, and dread. By the time I got to the school door, I started to break down and cry.

My grandfather, my father's father, lived with us at that time and he accompanied me to school that first day together with my mother. He was a man with a thick black beard, a really patriarchal-looking person. I was never close to my grandfather. I was afraid of his beard. But I remember grabbing hold of him and not letting go because I didn't want to go to school, or for him to leave me. I knew my mother wanted to throw me to the school wolves, for she had always told me that school was important.

There were a number of reasons for my fear and apprehension. I was going to a place that was completely foreign to me. I had lived for five years in an environment where the only language of discourse was Yiddish, and I knew virtually no English. To be sure, my father was forced to use English in the store with the Italian and Irish customers, but they were few and far between.

My first teacher was a young woman by the name of Miss Makeroff, blonde and blue-eyed, obviously not Jewish, and she obviously did not know any Yiddish. Here I was, with all my other Yiddish-speaking friends. We were bawling all over the place, every one of us, I remember, and couldn't make ourselves understood. There was one little black child in there too. We were an integrated school—one little black child.

The black child was the son of a "super" or superintendent, the person who performed all the maintenance in apartment houses in return for free rent and some minimal payment. Since that black child had no one to play with but us Yiddish-speaking kids, he spoke Yiddish too. Why not?

Miss Makeroff immediately started teaching us things like how to use our handkerchiefs, as if we didn't know. She assumed we were all coming from a kind of primitive environment that was without any kind of culture. She assumed she and the public school system were rescuing us from the depths of depravity. She was there to save us from the worst evil.

In any case, I overcame my first days, weeks, even months of fear, loathing, and resentment and got to like the school for some strange reason. I started speaking a language I thought the rest of America was speaking and I began to fit in.

This was a competitive place. Elementary school, yes. Can you imagine elementary school being competitive? I'll never forget Mrs. Katz, who was the mother of Martha Katz, who was one of my classmates, coming into the candy store and telling my mother—of course, in Yiddish—that her Martha was able to get higher grades than I could. My mother said that's impossible, just impossible.

My mother had her revenge at sixth-grade graduation. She wasn't going to come. She was busy in the store, but I told her to come anyway. I received the award as the leading student in the school, PS 23. By then, my English was impeccable and I was the valedictorian for the sixth-grade graduating class. Martha Katz sat there and her mother was gloomy. My mother said to her, "You see!" It was very competitive.

I then went to James K. Paulding Junior High, which was, as I remember, about a four-mile walk from my apartment. Or it felt that way. I vividly do remember one event happening while I was on my way home from junior high one day. I looked up in the sky and I saw a dirigible flying with a Nazi swastika on its tail. The German *Hindenburg* passed right over the Jewish neighborhood in the Bronx, right over. I can imagine all of the Bronx looking up there and cursing. I immediately said, "May it burn in hell." And a few hours later it did, in one of the greatest aerial so-called disasters of all time. Not to me.

It burned because we willed it to burn, I'm sure. When we listened that evening to the radio reporter bewailing the terrible tragedy, we thought, "What kind of nonsense is that?" It was the greatest victory of mankind over the devil we'd ever seen. We won! I remember that one political thing that happened while in junior high school.

When I finished junior high school, I had a choice of going to one of two high schools. I could have gone to the neighborhood school, which was Morris High School, the one that most of my friends and, later, former Secretary of State General Colin Powell went to. But I took special examinations and I was qualified by passing the examination and by my school grades to go to either Townsend Harris High School or Stuyvesant High School.

The New York Board of Higher Education established Townsend Harris Hall. It existed only into the early 1940s, when Fiorello La Guardia, the populist mayor, decided it was too elitist and had to be closed. It was a high school for young boys only and it was run by City College. It was a formidable academy and was actually on the City College campus. By the way, it's since reopened and is ranked among the best public high schools in the nation.

The other place was Stuyvesant High School in downtown Manhattan, and that's the school I chose because I wanted to be in the downtown area. It was a more exciting area and was easier to get to from the Bronx than the City College campus in Queens. More importantly, most of my friends who made it into the elite high schools were going to go to Stuyvesant rather than Townsend Harris. Those going to Townsend Harris we thought were goofy kids. They were more into Latin and Greek, and we were modern as Stuyvesant focused primarily on sciences, math, and technology, and with a good humanities base too.

It was an excellent, perhaps a remarkable, school for being a public high school. Politically, that was where I was involved with the forming of the American Student Union, which was linked to the Communist Party. But that activity didn't interfere with my studies or my classes.

For me, high school wasn't a social experience. It was more an intellectual experience and the location of my secular education. The rest of my education was occurring among left-wing Jewish organizations such as Mittelschule, which was affiliated with Camp Kinderland, a summer camp that would become an integral part of my political maturity, and the Jewish People's Fraternal Order, which was another Communist-influenced organization of young people. In fact, Camp Kinderland eventually led to my being mentioned before the House Un-American Activities Committee, or HUAC, in 1955.

A number of teachers at Stuyvesant did have an impact on me. There was one teacher of English literature who was one of the editors of the *New Leader,* a Social Democratic weekly. He was the drama and film critic, and although we politically disagreed, aesthetically we agreed.

He's the one who introduced me to film aesthetics, and I introduced him to the quality of the Yiddish art theater. I was involved in acting in amateur productions in my Yiddish schools and through them became active with the Yiddish workers' theater movement, out of which came some prominent Broadway and Hollywood performers and creative artists.

A notable experience I had in Stuyvesant—actually, I was sitting at home on December 7, 1941, doing my homework—was listening to the New York Philharmonic radio broadcast when it was interrupted by an announcement about the attack on Pearl Harbor.

To be sure, by that time I was gung-ho for World War II. Most people didn't think what came to be known as "Pearl Harbor Day" was a great day, but I thought it was. It got the United States more involved in the war, which was a war for the fatherland, the fatherland not being the United States but the Soviet Union.

I graduated from Stuyvesant in January 1942 and went on automatically to City College. It was expected that from Stuyvesant, for a child of immigrants, including small retail merchants and the working class, there was no other choice but one of the city colleges. If you were going to go to college, it would be City College or Brooklyn College or Hunter College. The city colleges were free and with remarkable faculties, a good number of whom were Jews who couldn't get jobs anywhere else. To me, that was the reason City College had a remarkable faculty.

I entered City College as a chemistry major. Why not? I came from a technically oriented high school. All of my work was in sciences and mathematics. I went into City College already having had differential calculus. But my first stint at City College lasted just a year and a half, until June 1943. That eighteen months, I took a lot of chemistry, a lot of biology, math, and German. I don't know why I took German. I must have had a sense that I was going to need it sometime or other.

It was a time of political turmoil at City College. Between 1940 and 1942, the Rapp-Coudert Committee investigated Communist activities in the city universities, primarily Brooklyn and City College. There was a strong Communist Party faction among the faculty in City College and to a lesser extent at Brooklyn College, and they were all purged after these hearings, which were a local counterpart to the House Un-American Activities Committee, the more famous Communist inquisition committee.

One of the first classes I had as a freshman was a German class, and I remember the German professor was a feisty little man who was not going to take any crap from anybody. Obviously, organizationally, he wasn't involved in anything because he was still there teaching.

"You're coming into a university where academic freedom no longer exists," he told us. "All the good people were fired."

Some of us wise guys at City College asked, "If all the good people were fired, then what the hell are you still doing here?"

"If they come after me, I beat them over the head."

"Who are the they?" we said.

"The Rapp-Coudert shit." Those were exactly the words he used.

He was right about who was purged because some great scholars went on to other great places and great things. They were the leadership of the City College teachers' union, which was Communist dominated. Among the most prominent people who were eliminated by Rapp-Coudert were the Foner brothers, Philip and Jack, two great historians who did good work despite being blacklisted. There was Morris Schappes in the English Department, who went on to become the editor of *Jewish Currents,* and Moses Finkelstein, who left to teach in England and actually became Sir Moses Finley after he changed his name.

There was still a cadre of faculty who were significantly vibrant, independent, and actively involved in scholarship, and I learned a lot from them. But "the Rapp-Coudert shit" was not a good sign of things to come for the nation or the left.

Political Education (Also Known as Summer Camp)

Long before college, my political and cultural education—and that of other Jewish kids I knew—was formed in the Yiddish schools. They became the major activity of many Communist Party people because they were seen as the means by which their ideas and culture could be transmitted to the future. The Yiddish schools were almost communal institutions, promoting cultural pluralism and autonomy for Jewish people. Yiddish was considered a central instrument in preserving values among the Jewish people. The language was at the core of the culture. There were a number of ideological segments of the Yiddish school movement.

The first schools were founded by the more moderate Workmen's Circle in the pre–World War I period. But by the 1920s, the split in the socialist movement between Communists and non-Communists led to a breakup in the Yiddish school movement, and a summer camp called Camp Kinderland became a key cultural component of the schools. It was taken over by the Communist Party.

Of course, my parents sent me to the Yiddish school that was run by the International Workers Order, or IWO. In about 1925, the International Workers Order became a central instrument of party policy among immigrants and the children of immigrants. The IWO was an insurance and beneficial society that broke off from the anti-Communist Workmen's Circle. These organizations were mutual aid societies, providing life insurance, health insurance, unemployment compensation, and burial benefits, among others.

The IWO not only focused on Jewish immigrants. It also organized aid societies for Croatians, Poles, and others. The strategy was that there could be autonomous cultural expression within the framework of the totality of the United States. Frankly, this is a principle I would embrace years later when I helped to form all the ethnic studies programs at the University of Minnesota. In my view, autonomous cultural expression is critical for the freedom of all groups.

When I was six or seven, my parents enrolled me in the Yiddish school, which I attended later in the day after public school. As soon as you enrolled you became a member of the Young Pioneers of America, or YPA, which was the Communist youth group. Everything we did was in Yiddish. All the pledges were in Yiddish. We sang the "Internationale," the left-wing anthem, in Yiddish. We put on red bandanas as members of YPA. The uniforms we wore and the whole cultural ambience of the Young Pioneers I saw completely reproduced when I went to China a half century later. It was a kind of mirror image of what we were doing in the Bronx, just not in Yiddish.

I graduated into the Young Communist League, or YCL, at the age of thirteen or fourteen. It was kind of an automatic progression. It was as if you were on a treadmill—you couldn't do anything about it. The YPA and YCL were very much engaged in the Yiddish cultural movement. We even had our own theater that laid the foundation for a little bit of acting I did later in life. These were more than just afternoon schools where you were taught Yiddish. We were also taught the social sciences—that is, Marxism, Leninism, Stalinism.

We put on the wall important articles from the press. The press was always the *Freiheit* and the *Daily Worker,* but the *Freiheit* was in Yiddish. The whole atmosphere was, there's going to be a Soviet America the day after tomorrow. The revolution is going to come. Look, the Great Depression is here. Everything that was predicted by the great Marxist theoretician, Joseph Stalin, is coming true. The crisis in the capitalist world is increasing. The contradictions are growing and the conflicts between the imperialist powers are getting stronger, so the revolution is going to come any moment. But, obviously, our great enemies are the socialists and the social fascists and the Trotskyites. That was the position I took when I was seven years old.

Did I know what I was doing? Of course not.

This political education became even more intensified in the summer months when we transferred all our activity to twenty-four hours a day, seven days a week at Camp Kinderland, the Yiddish-speaking summer camp for the children of Communist-leaning parents.

But even before Camp Kinderland, my parents wanted me to have a secular experience, a non-Jewish experience, so in 1936 or 1937, they sent me to Camp Wo-Chi-Ca, which was short for Workers' Children's Camp. It was an experience, I'll tell you. It was the first time I ever had bacon. And I happened to get a counselor who was not only a Communist but also a nudist. We were all naked.

It was also the first time I saw Clarence Hathaway, which means he was probably the first person I ever met from Minnesota. Hathaway was a leader of the Communist Party nationally and in Minnesota, and then the editor of the *Daily Worker.* He came to talk to us eleven- and twelve-year-old campers, but he was drunk. From that I learned that Party leaders sometimes need a drink.

Little did I know that he was going to be expelled from the party for excessive drinking or that, in one of my first years at the University of Minnesota, I'd go out for a summer camping interlude with a group of my friends only to meet Hathaway again, soon before he died.

Wo-Chi-Ca was billed as a camp for non-Jews. But to be sure, since it was in upstate New York, its clientele was largely from the metropolitan New York area, and it was probably mostly Jews, but non-Yiddish-speaking Jews. These were the second-generation assimilated ones, in contrast with Camp Kinderland, where I'd spend many of the next years of my summers as both a camper and a counselor.

In 1939, at the age of fourteen, I was at Camp Kinderland when we learned about the Nonaggression Pact between the Soviet Union and Germany, which seemed like an odd partnership. I remember vividly that, up until August 1939, we were carrying on camp activities that were antifascist and anti-Nazi and that were connected with the whole anti-Nazi movement.

At that moment, when the Nonaggression Pact was signed, I remember there was immediate confusion, particularly among the campers. I assume it was among the counselors and party activists too. That confusion lasted less than a day in my recollection. We quickly came to the conclusion that this was the best thing that ever happened. The imperialist West was out to destroy the Soviet Union by refusing to enter into a kind of alliance. What the Soviet Union was doing was preempting any kind of attack through the Nonaggression Pact with the Nazis. This was really a concealed anti-Nazi move. And we bought it.

Two years later, when Germany attacked the Soviet Union, it did not lead me to any reconsideration. To the contrary, it confirmed what we believed to begin with. In effect, that two years had given the Soviet Union time to rearm and to strengthen its position, to get rid of what they called the Finnish fascists in the North, during the so-called Winter War, and to get rid of the Japanese fascists in the East. We took care of all of them between 1939 and 1941. It strengthened the Soviet Union.

Obviously, we were living in a world of illusion. That same illusion continued to build for me over the next decade.

Around that time, we at Stuyvesant High School who were in the Young Communist League organized around many activities, calling ourselves the American Students' Union. In 1942 we organized and helped in the campaigns for Communist Party candidates who were running as American Labor Party candidates for city council positions. We campaigned against those whom we deemed to be either insufficiently anti-Nazi or exceedingly anti-Semitic.

I consistently got a sense of satisfaction from all of this activity. If I hadn't, I wouldn't have done it. After all, I was bringing the day of the revolution closer with every one of those things I was doing.

My relationship with my parents in regard to all this was very close, very supportive. Most kids rebel against their parents. I didn't, or at least I didn't seem to. I adopted their political outlook quickly. Through my reading I was convinced that not only was I right and my parents were right, but we had scientific justification for everything we were doing. We were the owners of a rational view of society. Everybody else was irrational. That's what happens when you read *Das Kapital* in Yiddish when you're ten years old.

After World War II, the shuls and camps began to lose their clout. I think it came from those who always felt that proletarian internationalism meant the elimination of cultural difference. I don't know if the leaders in New York were acting primarily on their own. Or if it was because of the policy in the Soviet Union they called "rootless cosmopolitanism," which was code for anti-Semitism against, mostly, Jewish artists in the Soviet Union.

But the IWO had, at its height, a membership of about two hundred thousand all over the United States, and even in Minnesota. For example, Minnesota governor Rudy Perpich's parents were members of the Croatian fraternal organization of the IWO. Perpich's first medical insurance was through the IWO. He became a dentist, in the hope, his father said, that he could be an IWO dentist. I'm pointing this out to show that this wasn't just a New York or East Coast thing, but even in Minnesota the IWO was an important institution.

Looking back, Camp Kinderland was a hothouse of all kinds of left-wing activities. It was a place of remarkable cultural significance. Artists like Aaron Copland and Marc Chagall would visit and teach. As a camper I benefited from this. Later, as a counselor, I was able to mold my kids, but never did I try to get them to join the Communist Party. I never did that, but I did try to influence them. It wasn't that I didn't want to recruit them. I just didn't think that at the age of twelve or thirteen they were capable of independent judgment. Sure, to be in the Young Communist League or Young Pioneers is one thing, but to be a member of the party, no. My own movement into party organizations took place when I was quite young, and I guess I wasn't in a position to make a mature decision either. I was just my father's and my mother's son, but, when I got older, I didn't want to play that role of recruiting kids at the camp.

This reluctance to recruit children into the Communist Party would serve me well when the House Un-American Activities Committee began investigating Camp Kinderland a few years later. My name was mentioned, but I dodged a big bullet.

I guess, too, I was somehow anticipating the path of my parents. Their aspirations for me were always to move out of the working class but to retain a kind of ideological commitment to the working class. In the last years of their lives, however, they became disillusioned with the international events, particularly in the Soviet Union. They never really found a new ideal to take the place of the old, an ideal that became horribly tarnished.

Saved by Hernias

I stopped going to Camp Kinderland in the summer of 1943 when I was drafted into the army. There was no question. At age eighteen, you registered for the draft, and the way things were going in Europe and in Asia, if you registered, you were drafted, and if you didn't have flat feet or some kind of mental disability, you became a soldier. Actually, even if you had a mental disability you were drafted. For flat feet they might kick you out. There were many people with mental deficiencies in the army, but I never saw anyone with flat feet.

The Communist Party was neither encouraging nor discouraging men about joining the army. This was a private decision that people made. More likely than not they would enlist, but I was on the young side. The question of my being a member of the party was never raised by the army. Actually, hardly anybody knew it. I wasn't officially a member of the party. I was in the Young Communist League. The army was never interested in my politics. Nothing came up about that, ever.

That point in the war, the spring and summer of 1943, was the peak of the need for cannon fodder. I went through basic training in the infantry school at Fort Benning, Georgia, which was the most rigorous basic training one could go through if you weren't a marine. Then I was immediately assigned to the Army Special Training Program, or ASTP.

This was a unique program that sought to get army personnel from various top universities, train them in either languages or pre-med or engineering, and prepare them for technical skills in the army. Even though we were in the ASTP, we were required to take fundamental basic training in infantry, the hardest kind. The Fort Benning infantry training was the most physical and most soul-destroying experience I ever went though.

People who were with me were college students, freshmen, sophomores, some even juniors who were drafted at that particular time, and they were mainly from City College, Brooklyn College, Harvard, and Princeton. In other words, the elite of the elite, and physicality was not one of the characteristics of this group. The training personnel did not know how to cope with this group. They used the usual tactics of intimidation, but that didn't work. It was a thirteen-week basic training program. I think in those three months, I lost twenty pounds and gained a degree in intellectual stupidity, which has taken me a lifetime to overcome.

Being in Columbus, Georgia, the first time out of the New York area for me, was culturally mind boggling. We would spend all week in this kind of physical torture. Then for recreation they would give us a two-day pass to go to Columbus, where there were nothing but bars and whorehouses. For a bunch of intellectuals, who were looking for libraries and museums, this didn't make any sense. After a while, we'd spend our two-day passes in the barracks reading books, which the officers of the training group couldn't understand at all. "Why ain't you out gettin' drunk and gettin' laid?" is what they would shout at us. We said we are more interested in getting knowledge. They didn't understand that at all.

At the end of the thirteen weeks, one task was parachute jumping. My heart was in my mouth. Twice. Everybody had to do it twice, once for practice and once for the real thing. It didn't make any difference to me one way or the other. They both were the real thing. First they told you how to do it, then sent you up there to do it, and then they told you what you did wrong. It didn't happen to any of our people, but sometimes if you did it wrong, you never did get a second time, if you know what I mean.

Ultimately, they divided us ASTP guys into groups to go to different colleges. One group went to Ohio State University. Another group went to the University of California, Berkeley. It was my good fortune to be sent to the cream of the crop, the University of Dayton. The University of Dayton was a Catholic school. Dayton isn't the greatest place in the world and the university is not the greatest university.

For some strange reason, my testing in the army said I was most capable of being either a doctor or a translator. I was hoping to go in either direction, but before I even got settled in Dayton, the ASTP program was terminated. Subsequently, I learned that it was General Omar Bradley who canned ASTP on the grounds that the European theater would need replacement soldiers. So we were dispersed, and I was sent to the 102nd Ozark Division, which was then at Camp Swift, Texas. Camp Swift is in the hill country outside Austin, wonderful, beautiful country.

I spent weekends in Austin, and of course, at the University of Texas campus. Somehow or other, I got tied up with a Jewish retail merchant, who had a daughter, who was a student at UT, and he took me in. My mother felt all along that the merchant was actually what we call in Yiddish a *shadchan,* a matchmaker. But I don't know. I wasn't a good pick, not for an upper-middle-class, driven Jewish Texas merchant's daughter.

Nonetheless, I spent weekends with them. I stayed over at their house. I dated his daughter. We went to events at the university. I spent a lot of time reading in the university library. Meanwhile, the powers that be at Camp Swift discovered that I had German training at City College. Apparently, at that point my division was scheduled to participate in a secondary invasion of France after D-Day. Obviously, we would be hooking up with German troops, so they needed someone in divisional headquarters who spoke German, or who could at least understand it. All of a sudden, I found myself going from a Browning automatic rifle man, or BAR-man, to a crash course on military intelligence and how to interrogate. So while all my friends were practicing how to kill people, I was practicing working on improving my German. Apparently, once we went overseas, I would have been shifted to divisional headquarters, to be either an interpreter or a translator, but it never happened.

On D-Day I was in Camp Swift when the announcement was made that Allied forces had landed on the Normandy beaches, and I remember all of us being glued to the radio, twenty-four hours a day that day. Within a few weeks we left Camp Swift for Fort Dix, New Jersey, outside Trenton, where we were on further training and in preparation for overseas shipment.

In the course of that training, I was on a bit of maneuvers in the pine counties of New Jersey, when all of a sudden I felt a sharp twinge in my right side. It was a little pain, but you get over it and I forgot about it.

Prior to going overseas, we all received a thorough physical examination to make sure we were healthy enough to be killed. In the course of this physical examination, it was discovered that I had, in fact, a severe hernia. I knew I had discomfort down there, but I thought everybody had discomfort down there. As my friends were getting ready to move out to battle, I was sent to the Fort Dix hospital for a double hernia operation.

Nowadays, a hernia repair is nothing. You go in, they cut you up, and you go out. In those days it was a big deal. They put me in the hospital for two days before I had the operation and then I was there for weeks recuperating, which was fine with me. I was already ambulatory when the division was pulling out of Fort Dix. I remember coming out of the hospital to visit all of my friends, some of whom I'd known from City College, from the University of Dayton, and others I got to know at Camp Swift. We were a close-knit group, mostly Jewish. For some odd reason, the Ozark Division had mostly Jewish infantrymen, all, of course, very highly educated, college trained, but all infantrymen.

I remember spending the last night or two with some of them before they left. Some said, "Oh, you are so lucky you are not going to go overseas." Others said, "Too bad you are not going to be with us."

It was the last I saw of them, and for that matter, the last anybody saw of them because my group, the divisional headquarters group, was wiped out. Every one of my friends was killed. If I had gone along with them, we wouldn't be talking now. I'd be dead.

My life was probably saved by my hernias.

What do you do with a guy with a recovering double hernia, who's an infantryman and who knows German? You send him to the air force, of course. Remember, the air force was then part of the army. They sent me, of all places, to Seattle, Washington, and the Boeing aircraft factory, where I was to learn the intricacies of the B-29 superbomber that was then coming into production to be used for dropping the atomic bomb. We didn't know there was an atomic bomb at the time. I did learn how to take apart the engine.

There was another reason for going there. They thought there was a German spy ring there, and I was to infiltrate and get any kind of information out of them. I didn't find a spy ring. The only thing I found was a bunch of beer-guzzling Germans who were working at Boeing, and I joined them for nightly beer-drinking parties. They spoke German, but they were not Nazis. Yes, the only time I used my German in the army was in bars with drunken Germans. I was then sent to Keesler Air Force Base in Biloxi, Mississippi, where I took care of B-29s and did some incidental German translation. I worked on the engines, which may be why they crashed.

One of the things about being down in Biloxi is you can easily get to New Orleans. In Biloxi I came into contact with a minor Communist Party official who was in the army, who was from New York, who knew me, and I knew of him. We had long weekends and we spent them in what the party would consider productive activity. We'd go to New Orleans, to the National Maritime Union headquarters, and help with their organizing campaigns.

On the way, we'd go on the famous New Orleans trolleys. In those days, the backseats of the trolleys had planks that could be moved from seat to seat that said "Colored Only." We'd move to the back, take these planks off, and throw them out the window. This was our private campaign against segregation or apartheid. We were fighting the party's battle for racial equality.

It was while I was at Keesler that the war came to an end. By March 1946, I was discharged from the army, and the next chapter, the next transition of my life, began. I was completing my undergraduate degree, moving on to graduate school, getting married, and, as I learned more, coming to a deepening realization that I was praying to a false god, the god of Soviet policy and ideology.

2 Leaving the Party, Entering the Academy

When World War II ended, after I was demobilized from the United States Army and before I went back to City College to finish my undergraduate degree, I was at leisure. It was now 1946. I took great advantage of what was called the "52-20 Club." That was a provision in the GI Bill that allowed demobilized service people to receive fifty-two payments of twenty dollars a week until returning to school or getting a job.

So for about three months before heading back to City College, I got twenty bucks a week, which in 1946 was a fortune, particularly when I was living at home. I mean, the subway still cost a nickel to ride. A Nathan's hotdog was a nickel. The Horn & Hardart automat had sandwiches for ten and twenty cents. I was among those who are inclined to the national pastime of baseball, so from April or May until June, I spent three or four days a week at either Yankee Stadium or the Polo Grounds, and with very good tickets, very good seats right behind the bullpen. To be sure, it was in the bleachers and it was less than a dollar, so I could afford it, and I saw memorable games, including Bobby Feller of the Cleveland Indians pitch a no-hitter against the Yankees.

It was just wonderful, the best time of my life. I wasn't married, I had no obligations, I didn't have to go to school, and I had no political assignments. Yes, I was involved with the Joe York Club of the Communist Party at the time, but I was still playing around a little bit while strengthening my contact with the Yiddish theater movement and, particularly, with Yiddish actors.

One of the odd jobs I was able to pick up was performing in Yiddish commercials on the Yiddish radio station, WEVD. That was the social-ist station named after Eugene V. Debs. I was particularly happy about one Alka-Seltzer commercial, which became fairly well known. It was so well known that many years later, when the distinguished cultural historian Larry Levine of the University of California, Berkeley, came to the University of Minnesota campus to lecture, he remembered listening to it. At that point all of my colleagues in the History Department—most of whom were not Jewish and didn't know a word of Yiddish—insisted that I give the commercial. I remembered it by heart—and Larry Levine then gave the lecture.

The commercial went something like this:

Hot ir kop-fardreyenish? Boykh farshtopenish? Yesurim in di gedirim? Ir hot?
Den nemt a glezl vaser. Leygt arayn a tablet alke-seltser.
Zh-zh-zh.
Hert er misht musirn musirn. Azoy geyt bay aykh in boykh, musirn musirn.
Oy s'iz kop-fardreyenish! Oy s'iz boykh farshtopenish! Oy s'iz yesurim in di gedirim!
Koyft alke seltser!

You want the translation?

Do you have headaches? Stomachaches? Troubles all around?
You do?
Then grab a glass of water. Put in a tablet of Alka-Seltzer.
Pfzz, Pfzz, Pfzz.
Listen to it bubble and fizz.
Just like it will in your stomach, bubble and fizz.
Oy, it's a headache! Oy, it's a stomachache! Oy, it's general pain!
Buy Alka-Seltzer!

And that was the highlight of my commercial voice-over career.

Meanwhile, my whole attitude toward academic discipline had changed. When I went back to my first chemistry class at City College after coming out of the army, I was given a chemistry manual and told to follow it. In the middle of the first class, I shouted out, "I didn't come to college to learn to be a glorified cook," because that's what I was doing. I was following recipes. The professor looked at me and he said, "Mr. Berman, I don't think you have the temperament to be a chemist," and I looked at him and said, "You know, Professor, I think you're right," and I walked out.

I discovered that the sciences were not for me, not because I couldn't handle them, but because they didn't answer the questions I was most interested in. They couldn't help me look at the world and try to change it. The answers I wanted could mostly be found by going into the historical record, so I switched to history. What do they say? The rest *is* history.

I had all this experience both in the movement, in Camp Kinderland, the Yiddish stuff, and the army, and I was into historical thinking. I enrolled in a few history classes and found out it was fascinating and had the teachers who made it fascinating. I also had some teachers who made it dull. But there was Joseph Wisan, a history of journalism guy, who helped me, and who went on to become the History Department chairman. There was Michael Kraus, a really distinguished American historian, and, of course, Richard B. Morris, who later went on to Columbia and was a wonderful legal historian.

So I became a history major, but how you get a job with a history degree remained a mystery. I had, as a member of the Depression generation, thought of going into high school teaching because the need to make a living was more important to me than anything else. Consequently, in my last years at City College I took pedagogy courses and did the preliminary work toward licensure as a high school social sciences teacher.

It was at that point that they told me that I wouldn't be able to pass the speech exam because I had too much of a New York accent and that I had to go take speech therapy. I went to the speech therapy class. In those days they had recordings on vinyl, and the recording they gave me to practice speech on was a recording of—you're not going to believe this—Hubert Humphrey's famous civil rights speech at the 1948 Democratic National Convention. His speech was considered standard English and mine wasn't.

Who could have imagined that Hubert Humphrey would teach me how to speak standard English? Or who could have known that years later I'd actually share a University office with Hubert? When I told Hubert about my speech therapy, he was so proud. But as far as I can tell, I still have my New York accent.

Actually, I had another choice besides high school or college teaching. I was leaning toward going into the theater. I did get a scholarship to New York's American Academy of Dramatic Arts, a famous place. Anybody who was anybody went to it. I went a couple of weeks, on weekends only. Then they told me I had to come every day if I really wanted to accomplish anything. Coming every day meant I would have to give up my graduate work. I had a choice there. I stuck with teaching.

But many years later, when I was described at my retirement dinner as the "Zero Mostel of historians," that wasn't very far off the mark. I looked up to Zero Mostel. He came out of City College too.

My injection of humor into my work as a historian came naturally. I think I did that right from the start in my undergraduate years, and for a long time I didn't notice what I was doing. I first became aware of it when I did a televised public history course on Channel 2 in the Twin Cities. People would tune in and stay tuned in. Humor is a very important ingredient in keeping an audience, and I used it very effectively in my classroom lectures as well. There was always a little bit of Yiddish theater in my lectures.

Breaking from the Party

I graduated from City College in 1948. Joe Wisan called me in and said, "How would you like to stay here in a staff position?" By then I knew I wanted to go on to graduate school. "What would I do?" I asked. "You'd be a reader, a grader." I'd also be a chief cook and bottle washer, boot shiner, and all that kind of stuff, but it sounded good to me, so I stayed on through the '48–'49 school year.

While I was doing my first year of graduate work at Columbia, I was also doing what I guess you would call today a teaching assistantship at City College. I taught night classes and had some of the most remarkable students, some of whom went on to become leading historians. In one of my freshman history classes, there were Seymour Drescher, one of the most distinguished economic and slavery historians in the United States; Leonard Dinnerstein, a wonderful historian of anti-Semitism; and Peter Sugar, a European historian. All in one class. I guess I was a good teacher.

They've told me that I had a great influence on getting them to go into the history profession, which is fine as far as those guys are concerned because they made out well. I hope I didn't get people into the profession who didn't make out well. That was a remarkable experience, really, to have kids like that in your first year of teaching. It was wonderful. I'd say something and they'd say, "You're full of shit." They were close enough to me in age that they could say that. More often than not, they were right, but, to be fair, I was teaching out of my discipline. I was teaching this freshman history class at City College that was essentially from cavemen to Truman. What did I know about cavemen or medieval society?

But even in my earliest days of teaching, I brought my concept of history to the students very simply by saying that history is not something that is permanently enshrined in stone. It is something that we are constantly evolving, discovering, evaluating, and reanalyzing. There are certain fundamentals that we use to try to understand history, and these fundamentals are the relationship of different groups to society and to themselves, and probably all of them are connected to the various forms of the means of production.

I was conscious of bringing in a Marxist interpretation of history. It was my interpretation. I couldn't keep it from them. There were quite a few people on the faculty at City College who had that interpretation. But some of them were less overt than the ones who were thrown out during the purge of the leftist faculty a few years earlier. I didn't have a Communist Party affiliation that would have made me vulnerable, so I was safe.

Around this time, my father decided that owning a candy store and being a small-business man didn't really fit with his image of what a proletarian activist should be. Still, his brother wanted him to become a partner in a saloon. That's not exactly progressive activism, I know, but for about a year or so he did that in Paterson, New Jersey, in a largely black neighborhood. A Jewish immigrant running a bar in an African American neighborhood in North Jersey is not a great dynamic.

That episode gave me an insight into corruption, a very good lesson. This is a part of immigrant experience that probably shouldn't be told, or at least the Jewish Community Relations Council wouldn't like it being told, but it was part of the experience.

Neither my uncle nor my father was a citizen, my father because of political reasons, but he finally did get citizenship, and my uncle because of his ties with the underworld. To have a bar, you have to have a license. To have a license, you have to be a citizen and not have ties with the underworld. So guess who owned the bar at Paterson? Me. Yes, I owned the bar in Paterson, or at least it was in my name, and eventually that bar got into some difficulties.

The Alcoholic Beverage Control agency down in Trenton questioned this. We were called in and went through a long hearing. My uncle and my father both made out as if they couldn't speak any English. I was the one who was interrogated. They asked how I could own a bar in New Jersey and still go to school in New York. I told them, well, yes, I lived in Paterson, but my official address was with my aunt and uncle in Brooklyn so that I could go to City College.

The ordeal over the liquor store and its rightful ownership came to a quick end through some kind of intervention, which I do not, to this day, understand. Let's just say the issue of the bar license was solved. This was a classic case of my uncle knew a guy who knew a guy. He had ties to some of the most interesting and most questionable characters in New Jersey, guys who made Tony Soprano look like a softie.

For example, the chief of police of Paterson was always in the bar. In fact, one time he asked me if I wanted to go with him and my father to a St. Louis Cardinals–New York Giants baseball game, and I said sure. We went from Paterson to the Polo Grounds and I found myself sitting in the box in the front row behind first base. That was with free tickets, and Stan Musial, the star player with the St. Louis Cardinals, the first baseman, walked over and started chatting with this chief, who introduced my father and me to him. It turned out that the chief of police was connected with all of the mobs of New Jersey and of New York, and my uncle was as well.

Eventually, my father got his citizenship just about that time, and my uncle did too. At that point, they relieved me of the onerous duty of being a bar owner. I turned the bar over to them. In a surprising development, it failed and they went out of business. But my father, given his politics, decided being a saloon owner was even more exploitative of the working class than owning a candy store. He said one of the problems about Jews in the world is that they are not productive.

How do you become productive? By going on the land. And what could a Jewish person who'd never been on the land before do? Well, back in the day, his father dealt with chickens in Lodz, Poland, so my father thought he knew chickens. He sold chickens, he plucked chickens, and he knew what chickens were about. He wasn't afraid of them, the way most Jews are afraid of little animals.

The Toms River–Lakewood, New Jersey, area was a large Jewish chicken farm community, many of whom were left-wingers. In fact, Communist Party members probably were there for the same reason my father gravitated to it—the belief that to regularize the occupational profile of the Jewish people it was necessary to get back on the land. It's the same motivation that motivated the Zionists, the kibbutzniks, though they put it in a collective way. Toms River also was a center of Yiddish radical cultural expression. There were choruses and dramatic clubs, community centers, and Communist Party activities of various kinds. I experienced it only indirectly because I was not on the farm myself, but I came almost every weekend. I'd help my parents out.

As a Jewish chicken farmer, my father became very active in the Farmers Union. When I came to Minnesota, which is a stronghold of the Farmers Union, and got to know some of the leaders of the Farmers Union, who happened also to be national leaders of the Farmers Union, they claimed they knew about my father. So I was always welcomed as a farm boy by the Minnesota Farmers Union. I didn't tell them that I was only there on weekends.

Chickens aside, as time wore on, many issues raised doubts in my mind about the Communist movement, but the first was when the debate began to become heated as to whether we were all doing the right thing in emphasizing Yiddish cultural autonomy, or whether we should move into an era of proletarian internationalism. In that new era, we'd stay away from all this provincialism of embracing Yiddish or Slovenian or Polish or whatever individual culture we identified with. It also began to dawn on me that some of the things I'd been hearing about what was happening in the Soviet Union might have some validity.

For example, I heard about the liquidation of the Polish leadership of the Communist Party by the Soviet Union around 1946 or 1947. But I heard about it long after it happened. Suddenly, Bolesław Bierut and Jakub Berman became leaders of the party. What happened? I learned that the leaders of the Polish party were just completely wiped out. Berman was somehow a distant relative of mine, a sort of second cousin or second uncle, or so my father said, but we didn't know him personally. He had been a longtime, but minor, leader in the Polish Communist Party. I think he cozied up to Stalin and got promoted. That a Jew could rise to power in anti-Semitic Poland at that time boggles the mind.

Anyway, I started hearing things like that. Then, one day in 1947, when I was teaching at the Mittelschule, I was walking along Eastern Parkway near the Brooklyn Museum with Aaron Bergman, who later wrote one of the first modern Yiddish-English dictionaries. He was the head of the Mittelschule, and obviously a good Communist Party man or he wouldn't have been in the position he had. All of a sudden, Aaron Bergman said to me, "They killed Izi Kharik."

First of all, who the hell was Izi Kharik? Izi Kharik was a well-known Yiddish poet in the Soviet Union. In 1938 his poetry stopped. He ceased publishing. He ceased to exist essentially. We never heard of him after that. Now, almost ten years later, Bergman told me, "They killed Izi Kharik."

"Who's they?"

"Stalin."

"Aaron, you're sounding like a right-wing nut."

"It's happened. I have to tell you. I've got information about it. I knew him. He was a friend. Before I came to the United States we went to school together."

"Why don't we say something about it?" I asked.

"It'll put ammunition in the hands of the enemy. We can't say anything about it." It all began to add up, but I wasn't sure to what quite yet.

At that same time, I first met Betty Silbering, who would become my wife. Betty is a Holocaust survivor. We met at City College at a sports field called Lewisohn Stadium. During the summertime that was the home of the New York Philharmonic Symphony. For seventy-five cents you could see the world's greatest musicians play. So, one day I went to this stadium and a sister of one of my friends came with a bunch of her friends. They all lived in what they called the "Girls' Club" in Brooklyn, which was set up by the Jewish Federation. It was a house for girls without families who came to New York. Betty lived there with her friends.

We began dating and I learned of her life as a Holocaust survivor and how her family perished. It's an incredible story. One aunt survived and went to Israel and Betty came to the United States. But Betty's mother perished in the Auschwitz gas chamber a few years after her father died in the Lodz, Poland, ghetto. When that ghetto was destroyed in August 1944, she went to Auschwitz and then to Stutthof, which was considered the worst of the concentration camps. And then to Dresden working in an armament factory during the fire bombing in February 1945.

Betty and her aunt got out alive by playing dead during a forced march from Dresden to who knows where. After a while, they simply knocked on a family's door and asked for help in Karlsbad in Czechoslovakia. There was a German family there that took them in and, when the Russians came to liberate the place, Betty and her aunt helped the German family dodge the Russians. Eventually, Betty made it to New York and, through a social service agency, made it to the Girls' Club. In March 1950 we were married.[1]

Through Betty I met many of the people who immigrated to the United States. They weren't in concentration camps the way she was, but they had been in the Soviet Union during World War II. Her best friend, Alex Feingold, his father was among them. He was an old Bundist whom I respected very much, and he started telling tales of what was happening, what he experienced in the Soviet Union. I called it *"bubbe meise."* That's basically an old wives' tale in Yiddish. I said to Alex, "It's all a bunch of crap. You had a bad experience and now you're blaming it all on the party." But I started hearing many things like that, and I started reading many things.

Meanwhile, doubts began appearing in my mind during the 1948 Henry Wallace campaign, when he was put up as the candidate for president on the Progressive Party ticket. It was essentially a campaign that was run by the Communist Party. I think it's fully acknowledged now

---

1. [I was able to fill in what Hy told me, and confirm the facts of Betty's story, with the assistance of the excellent book *After the Girls Club: How Teenaged Holocaust Survivors Built New Lives in America,* by Carole Bell Ford (Lexington Books, 2010).—J.W.]

that outside of Henry Wallace there were few non-Communists in the upper echelons in that campaign. I didn't articulate my doubts, but they started appearing largely because of the alienation of the labor movement. My belief then was that a Marxist movement, like the Communist Party, can go nowhere without at least some kind of loose ties and affiliations with the labor movement. But there was none in that Wallace campaign. That disturbed me.

Ultimately, it was the events of 1951 and '52 that caused my complete break with the party. It culminated with the anticosmopolitan campaign, which was the attack on Jewish intellectuals in the Soviet Union. And when artists or academics were attacked in the party press, their Yiddish or Jewish name was printed in parentheses, and here in the American Party press too.

I said, "What the hell is this all about? Why all of a sudden this?"

I started raising these questions and I was told to shut up, that there was a reason. There must be a good reason. The Cold War was then brewing and getting hotter and hotter. I began to start putting two and two together.

Then came the Rudolf Slánský show trial and execution in Czechoslovakia, which was another attack on Jews and those who believed in internationalism. It was about putting down any kind of criticism of the Soviet Union. These were people who fought in Spain against Franco. At that point, rationality left. This was irrational.

Another thing happened that I started putting together. What was happening in the Soviet Union was a refutation of the principle of cultural pluralism and cultural autonomy, which was the core of what had been the Leninist principle of the national question. The Soviet Union was not adhering to key Marxist-Leninist principles.

I had discussions of the Slánský trial with other party members. Their reaction was to start shunning me. I was becoming, in Yiddish, a *farreter,* a traitor. Others said I was swallowing the poison of bourgeois propaganda. My father said the same thing to me. My father said in Yiddish, "You're beginning to sound just like the *Forward.* What's the matter? You've become a disciple of Abe Cahan?" Abe Cahan was the editor of the *Jewish Daily Forward,* and he was the most fanatical anti-Communist in the Jewish movement. This was the view that most people I knew had, that the Soviet Union could do no wrong.

My actual break from the party came when I wrote a review of Solomon Schwarz's book *The Jews in the Soviet Union* for the journal *Historia Judaica*. It was published, ironically, in the summer of 1952. The reason I say "ironically" is that it was the exact month, almost the exact day—August 12, 1952—that Itzik Feffer, the leader of the Jewish Anti-Fascist Committee, and other defendants were executed in Moscow. I didn't know that was occurring then, but the death of the Anti-Fascist Committee, along with the Slánský trial, eventually became the events that pushed me over the edge.

My review was a repudiation of Soviet policy. It may read now as being subtle, but in 1952, for someone who was linked to the party, it was pretty clear what I was saying:

> The suppression of the last Jewish newspaper of any importance, the dissolution of the only noteworthy Jewish publishing house in the Soviet Union, and the impenetrable official silence on all matters of Jewish interest, permit only one interpretation. Sometime in 1948 it was decided to put an end to everything that in any way could stimulate or keep alive the national consciousness of Soviet Jews, so that they might ultimately disappear as a separate national group.
>
> Certainly, Jews will continue to live in the Soviet Union, and Jewish religious congregations may even exist, but there will be no "Jewry," no Jewish nation, no Jewish community or culture.
>
> Pessimistic as this statement may be, it is the evidence rather than personal bias that draws the author to this conclusion. The scholarship, the statistical charts, and the sober manner of presentation make this volume not only an important contribution to modern Jewish history, but also an important case study of national minority rights in a communist state.[2]

I didn't discuss it with anybody in the party before I published it. I knew that I couldn't. From then on, I was persona non grata, a *farreter*, a turncoat. Most party members I knew started shunning or, at least, ignoring me, but Edith Segal, who was the dance instructor and one of

---

2. Hyman Berman, book review of Solomon Schwarz's book *The Jews in the Soviet Union*, *Historia Judaica* 14 (1951): 84–87.

the icons at Camp Kinderland, saw me at a concert one night, and, as we were walking out of the hall, she yelled, "Traitor!"

A number of Jewish organizations were publicly denouncing the Soviet Union, but my parents were still alive and I just didn't want to become an activist on this particular issue. It would have meant, in effect, that I was saying I had been an idiot all along, and I wasn't publicly going to do that. I finally did that a full fifty years later in a public lecture in Minneapolis. Yes, it took me that long to personally and openly denounce communism. But for anybody reading between the lines, I had said it my *Historia Judaica* review. There was, however, nothing personalized in that review. I waited a half century for my personal denunciation.

The whole phenomenon of the Red Scare and House Un-American Activities Committee became a problem for me during those graduate school years. I was teaching in the evening session at City College, and someone—I've forgotten now who—came to me and said, "You've been mentioned in testimony given by Harvey Matusow."

Harvey Matusow had been a student at City College, was active in the Communist Party, left, and had turned as a witness for HUAC and at trials against alleged Communist trade unionists and others. He later recanted and wrote a book, *False Witness*. Anyway, apparently he mentioned me somewhere, although I've never been able to find evidence that that's the case.

The next thing I knew, I was called by the Higher Education Investigating Committee of the New York Committee on Higher Education, which was a Red-hunting enterprise headed by two former FBI agents. This was in late '52, after I had broken with the party. I went to an interview and was willing to talk about my activities, but nothing came of it.

Another contact was a few years after the *Historia Judaica* article, when the FBI came knocking on July 13, 1954, wanting to know about my activities and others'. I admitted to two agents that I was active in the Jewish People's Fraternal Order while at CCNY, that I attended and taught at Camp Kinderland, and that I knew about six men they mentioned whom I suspected were Communists. They left, and according to an FBI memo I received in my Freedom of Information Act files years later, the agents wrote:

Inasmuch as there is no evidence to indicate that the subject is affiliated with the CP [Communist Party], he is not being recommended for inclusion in the Security Index.

Since Berman has indicated a severance with the JPFO and other CP front groups, it is felt that he would not be a productive informant.

Geez, that sort of work on the part of the FBI makes me lose faith in their ability to sniff out a real troublemaker!

Years later, HUAC had hearings in 1955 having to do with Communist subversion in summer camps such as Camp Kinderland. The key witness they called was Herbert Gutman. Herb was a colleague of mine during our graduate years at Columbia and a friend, and he went on to become a wonderful scholar of African American history, among other topics. We'd known each other since working together as counselors at Camp Kinderland. Herb was called before HUAC as a hostile witness, and the guy who fingered him was also asked if he had other counselors besides Herb Gutman.

He said yes. He had me.

The witness against Herb and me was named Stanley Wechkin. Not sure what ever happened to him, but he is mentioned as the one who led the FBI to me for the 1954 interview, and here's how his testimony went about me. Not a whole lot, really. Wechkin was questioned by HUAC investigator Courtney Owens:

Owens: After your arrival at camp, were you assigned a group leader or section counselor or something of that sort?

Wechkin: Yes. I was assigned both a counselor and a group leader.

Owens: Who was your group leader?

Wechkin: Mr. Tobatchnikoff.

Owens: T-o-b-a-t-c-h-n-i-k-o-f-f?

Wechkin: Approximately.

Owens: Did you say you were also assigned a counselor?

Wechkin: His name was Chaim, C-h-a-i-m Berman, B-e-r-m-a-n.

Owens: Do you remember what other occupations, if any, Mr. Berman had?

Wechkin: I was told several years later, approximately 1951 or 1952, that Mr. Berman was an instructor in history at City College of New York.

Owens: Do you know whether or not he is still an instructor at City College?

Wechkin: I don't know. I imagine he is, though. Just one more thing: I also believe that he was an instructor at the Jewish People's Fraternal Order, JPFO, Mittelschule, in the Bronx.

Owens: In your opinion, Mr. Wechkin, was there any connection between Kinderland and the Jewish People's Fraternal Order's schools in New York City?

Wechkin: I was given to understand that Kinderland was a summer extension of JPFO schools in New York and Philadelphia.

Owens: Returning to your first summer at Camp Kinderland, other than the recreational facilities which we understand are available at these camps—and we will go into these things individually later on—what type of activity were you required to participate in as a camper?

Wechkin: There were classes in Jewish language and culture at Camp Kinderland, I believe, almost weekly or semiweekly.

Owens: What other activities?

Wechkin: Well, it all depends on what you consider the normal run of activities then. For instance, we would do a lot of singing. But we didn't do the kind of singing you get at most other camps. . . .

Owens: You constantly heard a knocking of the capitalist system of the United States. Is that correct?

Wechkin: Yes.

Owens: Just how would this line, so to speak, come about?

Wechkin: It was more or less an informal, person-to-person thing from a counselor to a camper or from a counselor to a group of campers. It wasn't anything organized. It was, as I say, informal, spontaneous almost.

Owens: Do you recollect whom you heard such statements from?

Wechkin: I remember some statements from my counselor, Chaim Berman, to that effect, although I don't recollect any individual statements.

Owens: Was this a continuous thing or sporadic?

Wechkin: It was spontaneous as the occasion demanded.

Owens: Could you elaborate a little more on what that line was?

Wechkin: If anybody had a question about any aspect of politics, economics and/or any of the social questions, and if we brought it to a counselor, he would more or less give it the Communist twist, or what I now understand to be the Communist twist.

Owens: At the time, however, you could not recognize it as the Communist Party line?

Wechkin: No, although I knew at that time that there was an element of Communism about Camp Kinderland.

Owens: How did you know that?

Wechkin: It is rather hard to say, but it more or less permeated the atmosphere there.

At that point, as I finished my Ph.D. and dodged the FBI, I wanted to escape from politics and just become a historian. It was time to concentrate on becoming a college professor.

The Academy

I don't think there was ever a time when I wasn't geared toward the academic world, or at least going into teaching. When you become a history major, what else is there for you to do? But there were hurdles to getting jobs in the 1950s.

The placement person in the Columbia History Department was a fellow named Shepard Clough, who said to me when I gave him my materials, "There are very limited places for you in the history profession. There are the city colleges and there are New York City high schools. Forget about anyplace else."

"Why do you say that?"

"Well, look in the mirror."

I looked in the mirror. "I don't look any different than you, Mr. Clough."

"You may not look different from me, but your name is different from mine."

In other words, overt anti-Semitism was still an integral and open part of the history profession. He said that he was simply warning me, rather than expressing it himself. "I don't like this," he said. "I am opposed to this, but this is the reality, and as placement officer I have to mention this."

That didn't make me feel any better.

Oh, it was a good thing to know, but things were changing. I think that was because of the major breakthrough in higher education made possible largely by the G.I. Bill. We would not have had the kind of influx of academic workers without the G.I. Bill. And City College, where I was an undergraduate, was not quite so Gentile as many other universities. Richard Morris, the great legal historian, was a mentor of mine at City College and encouraged me to dive into history as a profession. As it turned out, I followed him to Columbia for graduate school, and when I got there and was looking for an adviser to work with, he said to me, "You're not interested in colonial history or legal history, are you?" I said I wasn't. So he guided me to others on the faculty, which, if you think about it, was a who's who of great historians, the kind of guys whose textbooks everyone reads in college, or used to, anyway.

Morris said, "Why don't you go to Henry Steele Commager and speak with him." I went to Commager, who said, "I'm not interested in the labor movement. I'm a constitutional historian. Why don't you go to see Richard Hofstadter? He's interested in everything on the left." So, I went to see Hofstadter. "Yes," he said. "Labor history is something that would interest me, except I'm interested essentially in the history of ideas and you are interested in movements, and I don't think I would be the right person for you. Why don't you see Allan Nevins?"

I said, "Allan Nevins does Civil War stuff and industrial history." And Hofstadter responded, "Yes, but he's the closest that we have." So I bounced over to Nevins and he said, "I sympathize with you, but there's nobody here. The closest guy we have here is Harry Carman. He's an agricultural historian, not labor history, but he's got a soft heart and he's for the labor people, so I guess he may be interested in helping you." So I went to see Harry Carman and we hit it off immediately. In many ways, that changed the course of my career. Harry had a very interesting career development. He, too, came out of a different kind of setting than the Gentile scholar-teacher. He was an Upstate New York farmer, not from an upper-class farm but from a hardscrabble farm, who made it the hard way. He was guiding people into labor history because the others interested in that field were in the School of Business or the Economics Department. When it came to my links to Camp Kinderland and other Communist Party–related activity, I eventually viewed Harry as sort of my protector.

I was blessed with all of the great historians I could rub shoulders with. They were in the transitional generation of historians when I was at Columbia, men like Hofstadter, the great American intellectual historian, and Bill Leuchtenburg, the FDR scholar. And John Hope Franklin, the outstanding African American historian who was the chairman of the Brooklyn College History Department when I was teaching there while I was a graduate student at Columbia.

I must say, though, that over the course of my academic career, I saw tremendous changes. I think the biggest change, at least in the humanities and social sciences, was the expansion of the definition of who is being studied. In other words, when I was going through college, and then into graduate school, it was very rare to have someone like me study workers. It was very rare to have—well, John Hope Franklin studied blacks—but he was black, so he studied blacks. The fact of the matter is that most Americans were excluded from the discussion of American history.

What has happened since was this push that we believed in the full diversity of American society and that the full diversity of America should be studied. That's a big difference symbolized by this. One of the greatest historians whom I worked with when I was a student at Columbia was Nevins. He was, of course, a well-known American historian, but basically focused on the nineteenth century and the Civil War period. The interpretation of the Civil War back then was dominated by what was called the Dunning school, a group of historians who were basically apologists for slavery society. Because of my radical background I knew about W. E. B. Du Bois. So I picked up his book *Black Reconstruction*. It opened up my eyes completely, and I saw Reconstruction with a different and new perspective.

One day I ran into Nevins and told him, "I just read Du Bois's *Black Reconstruction*."

"You read that piece of junk?"

"Junk?"

"Remember, he's prejudiced, he's black, and not only that but he's also a Communist." Which he was, by the way. The point I'm making is that the whole profession was that way. It was close-minded. I don't think Nevins was a racist; he was just a typical American.

The individual scholar who had, I'd say, the most profound influence upon me was not an American historian but Salo W. Baron, the distinguished Jewish historian who worked into his nineties on his eighteen volumes of *A Social and Religious History of the Jews,* his magnum opus. He listened to all points of view. He once said to me, "I hope I live to write about the nineteenth century." Unfortunately, he didn't.

Baron was one of the most remarkable people I ever met in my life. He was quintessentially a scholar. He was European trained, at the University of Vienna. He had studied to be a rabbi and was the Miller Professor of Jewish History at Columbia University. He was a wonderful teacher. His seminar, which I took, was very personal, very close, very intellectually demanding.

I took Richard Hofstadter's seminar, which was really a very cold affair. I walked in; he'd give us an assignment and say, "I'll see you in ten weeks." I couldn't believe it. Look, I'm a labor historian and like to see the workers gain a lot of advantages, but this kind of advantage for a worker is too much. My understanding is that he did that all the time. That was his pattern of operation.

Baron, on the other hand, held his seminar after supper in his apartment. We would meet for two hours, for more than two hours sometimes. We met around a table, and Janet Baron, his wife, would set a sumptuous feast for us. We were treated not only to intellectual sustenance but also to good Jewish food. Baron's method of operation was that we ate, he would introduce a topic, present it, with bibliographical analysis, and then we would discuss it. When one of us gave a report, we, too, were required to do the same. Introduce a topic with a bibliographical analysis and then go into the essence of the argument. It was wonderful.

And as far as lecturing is concerned, Baron was my role model. He would come into the classroom without a single note and give the best-organized, most compact lectures I'd ever heard in my life. When I first saw him, I said to myself, "That's the way I want to do it when I become a professor." He was never the same any two times, always different, and that's the model I tried to use. I wasn't as successful as Baron, but I got the technique down.

Baron and I became really good friends, so much so that two or three years after the seminar he called me and asked if I would mind if he interviewed Betty for a job as his secretary. Betty was then working for the Federation of Jewish Philanthropies in downtown New York. My first thought was that this would be a conflict of interest and would somehow jeopardize my standing as a Ph.D. student. But Baron said, "Hy, there's no conflict of interest for you or me. You are not my student. I'm just on your doctoral committee. You are Harry Carman's student." Betty was qualified and got the job.

Soon after, it was time for my doctoral oral exam. It was an exam that tested you in every field that you focused on. In my case, that was Jewish history and U.S. history. Carman chaired it, and Commager, Hofstadter, and Morris were the American historians on the committee. Baron and Filip Friedman, a refugee scholar, were also on my committee. The exam was remarkable for a number of reasons. Halfway through the exam Carman received a telephone call from President Dwight Eisenhower, whom he was close to from Eisenhower's days as Columbia's president. So, in the middle of my doctoral exam, my adviser left and turned the chair over to Commager.

The second thing was that Richard Hofstadter started asking, out of nowhere, questions about Populist anti-Semitism. My knowledge of Populist anti-Semitism was limited to a couple of different sources. I said there is a long history and tradition of leftist anti-Semitism, and the Populists, I thought, didn't fit into that tradition because they were not really leftists. Rather, Populist anti-Semitism was probably a rural anti-Semitism, based on the belief in the "Jew banker," the so-called Rothschild image. He looked at me and said, "That's the first trenchant response I've gotten from all the doctoral exams I've given so far."

Then came Salo, whose first question was, "Tell me, Professor Berman, what was the condition of the Jews like in fifteenth-century Majorca?" Commager was astonished. "Salo, what the hell are you asking him?" Baron said, "If I didn't think he could answer that question I wouldn't ask it." I answered it and passed. But a funny thing happened afterward, a painful thing.

Right after the exam, Baron and Commager told me that when I was finished with my dissertation, they'd be happy to help me in the academic job market. Once upon a time, graduate school advisers actually used to place their students in positions around the country. Baron was always supportive, but I was primarily a U.S. historian, so Commager's recommendation would have been critical. Well, after I did finish my dissertation, I went to Commager during his office hours as I began searching for a job, and he looked at me and said, "Who are you? Never saw you in my life. Go." I left. That really hurt.

Many years later, I was already here at the University of Minnesota. Theodore Blegen, the great historian and one-time dean of the Graduate School, was retiring and there was to be a celebration in his honor. Lo and behold, Henry Steele Commager was one of the main speakers. He was in the History Department office and said to me, "Hello, Hy. Wasn't that fun when I threw you out of my office?" I looked at him and said, "You son of a bitch. You have no idea what kind of pain you caused me, and now you look upon that as a joke? You are an affront to this profession," and I walked out. I didn't care who he was. He deserved it.

Indeed, without that Commager recommendation, back in 1956 when I completed my Ph.D., here's what the job market looked like. We were at an American Historical Association meeting, I think in Washington, D.C., when Bill Leuchtenburg, who was really trying to help me out, said to me, "I've got a job interview for you."

"Oh, great. Where?"

"It's not the greatest place in the world."

"Yes? Where?"

"It isn't something that I'm proud of, either."

"Where? Where? Come on, tell me."

"It's General Beadle State College in Madison, South Dakota."

"Who?"

"General Beadle State College in Madison, South Dakota."

"Beggars can't be choosers."

"This is the person to contact for your interview."

I picked up the phone and called the guy, and got a time and place to meet him at his hotel room. I started wandering up to his room, and there was a mob of people there, maybe twenty to thirty. He probably had told everybody to come at the same time. He was going to save time. He opened the door, looked at the crowd, closed the door, a few minutes later opened the door, got on a chair, and started shouting.

"Anybody here who does not have a Ph.D. in hand, leave."

Half the people left.

"Anybody here who doesn't have a Ph.D. from . . ."

And then he started naming the prestigious universities—Harvard, Yale, Princeton, Columbia, Wisconsin. He did mention Minnesota. I remember that. "Leave!"

So, another half of the people went. That still left about twelve or thirteen of us. I was looking at this, and apparently what I was thinking was articulated. I wouldn't be caught dead at General Beadle State College in Madison, South Dakota. I turned around and started leaving and five other people followed me. I didn't even stay for the interview. Never found out who got the job.

Thankfully, soon after, I had two job offers but, stupidly, accepted both. That wasn't good. I was invited up to Bard College about three hours north of New York to speak in a colloquium of some sort. Apparently, there was an opening in the History Department there and my name was put forward, as was Irwin Unger's. He went on to win a Pulitzer Prize, by the way. Irwin, Irwin's wife, Betty, and I rode up on the train together, all four of us together. It was crazy.

As fate in life would have it, I was offered the job and not Irwin, and I tentatively accepted. I must say it was a tentative acceptance. It was just a one-year job and I accepted it with the proviso that if I got something that was tenure track or more than one year I'd take the other position. Within a week of accepting, John Hope Franklin offered me a job at Brooklyn College, and it was a three-year job. One-year job . . . three-year job. No doubt on that, but there was a catch: the three-year job may be tenure track or it may not be. I accepted Brooklyn College and the guy at Bard was really mad, but so what? We were happy to stay in New York, but this was a difficult time. During these three years, our first two children were born, Ruth in 1958 and Steve in 1959. So I had newly born children and was trying to get into the big swing of things professionally. It was an hour's ride from my apartment in the Columbia University area to Brooklyn College. I was teaching good students but was stuck in the night division, doing all the U.S. history. On the bright side, had I been in the regular daytime division I probably would have been stuck with five sections of the survey course. And me a beginner.

As it turned out, the Brooklyn College job wasn't a tenure track position. Franklin wanted to keep me, but college and department politics got in the way and I had to look elsewhere. Not to South Dakota this time. Franklin helped me get a position at Michigan State University in East Lansing.

Betty wasn't particularly happy. She loved New York. We had a great apartment on Riverside Drive, rent controlled at $104 a month. She finally kind of reconciled herself to leaving New York, and, somehow, I knew it was the best thing we ever did, getting out of New York.

I started at Michigan State for the academic year of 1960–61, and the deal was that I was to get tenure the very next year. One year and then tenure. Pretty good. But, unfortunately, it was not in the History Department. It was in what they called the American Thought and Language Department, or ATL. It was American studies essentially. It had certain disadvantages in a way because it was the general education function of Michigan State's undergraduate education. General education, then, was divided, as at many universities, into interdisciplinary programs. At Michigan State there was American Thought and Language, which was composition, literature, and history combined. There were the social sciences, and then there were natural sciences. I was in ATL. They were treating me very nicely, and the History Department came to me and asked me if I would teach a course for them. Michigan State would have been a good place for me to stay.

In less than a month we bought a house. We were going to stay there forever. But Betty was not happy. The house was in a place that had no sidewalks and it was within a short distance of the Michigan State stadium. Every Saturday during football season it was bedlam. Michigan State was the land-grant university and so had the agricultural college in Michigan. It was full of what I would call the red-faced farmer type, a shirt askew and the potbelly pushing out the buttons.

Remember, we came from New York. We'd go to the opera, to plays, to concerts almost every week. We lived in a beautiful seven-room apartment overlooking the Hudson River. And then, overnight, going from there to Michigan State was hard, and with two little kids. And no sidewalks. No sidewalks! It did not generate the kind of cultural richness that one would hope for.

I'm not complaining because we saw some marvelous things at Michigan State. We saw the Royal Ballet from London. Senator Barry

Goldwater came through and spent some time with us at Michigan State. It was, as we say in Minnesota now, interesting and different.

But in December 1960 at the American Historical Association meeting I ran into David Noble. David was the distinguished intellectual historian at the University of Minnesota whose tenure began in 1952. We'd met sometime in the mid-1950s at an earlier AHA meeting. We learned that we both had New Jersey connections. He came from a farm in Princeton, and my parents had that chicken farm in Toms River. That was the first thing that got us together. The second thing is we had comparable political outlooks at that time. He had left-wing Jewish friends from his army days, and we held comparable views about the nature of American history.

In 1958, at another historians' meeting, we really got to know each other, not talking about history so much as there was a National Football League playoff game between the New York Giants and the Baltimore Colts, probably one of the most famous playoff games prior to the NFL becoming a major icon in American culture. Rather than go to boring sessions at the AHA meeting, we decided to take the Sunday afternoon off, go to a bar, and watch the game. We had a ball and it was a great game. Three years later, he's the one responsible for getting me to the University of Minnesota.

Remember, I'd just been at Michigan State for three months then, September, October, November and into December. I ran into David and he said, "I think we're going to have an opening at the University of Minnesota, a joint position in history and social sciences. Would you be interested?" I said maybe, and soon after David invited me to Minneapolis to give a presentation. That's when I saw the stark racial differences in the workers at the airport between the Twin Cities and just about every other place I'd been.

My lecture was about the Great Railroad Strike of 1877, before many of these workers were represented by unions. It was a devastating, nationwide, violent strike of thousands of workers. I remember my talk vividly because I was filling in for a course on late nineteenth-century America. I forget who the instructor was, but I do remember very clearly that David Montgomery was the teacher's assistant, a Ph.D. student then, and David turned out to become one of the most distinguished labor historians of our time.

I finished the lecture and David Montgomery came over to me and praised the thing. He said, "Oh, we could really use you around here." I took it for what it was, a nice gesture, and I forgot about it.

Then, that evening there was a dinner at Harold Deutsch's house, the History Department chairman. Toward the end of the evening Harold came over to me and said, "You'll be staying with David Noble at his house on Commonwealth Avenue in St. Paul, and I'll come by Dave's house and pick you up at around nine o'clock and we'll go see the dean."

I looked at him strangely and asked, "Harold, what the hell do I want to see a dean for?" And he said, "Oh, don't you know we want you to stay? We're making you an offer." I guess I should have been more suspicious. The fact that I was asked to speak to a class and not to a more public, open lecture probably meant someone wanted to see how I did in a classroom setting. But I was still surprised.

The next morning I went to meet the dean, a fellow named Errett McDiarmid, who had been the University's chief librarian for many years. And there was no hemming or hawing. He wanted me to come join the History Department and work with the Social Sciences program, which they were actually slowly phasing out. I'd be tenure track, with an assurance I'd get tenure in a year or two. And I would be paid the princely sum of $8,000.

Of course, I had to talk with Betty about it. I picked up the phone and called her, told her of the offer, and she asked one question: "Do they have sidewalks in Minneapolis?" I said, "Yes," and she said, "Take the job."

When I got back to Michigan State, I told them I was moving, and they were shocked. They thought that at the very least I should have given them the opportunity to match the offer or to counter the offer, but I wasn't playing that game. The culture in the Twin Cities was so much more appealing to Betty and me.

In the fall of 1961, I came to the University of Minnesota. As you know, I never left.

3 Becoming a Minnesotan

When I got the invitation to come to Minnesota, I told John Hope Franklin and his reaction was the same as Harry Carman's when he heard the news. Both of them said, "I don't believe it." I asked, "What do you mean?" "That's one of the most bigoted departments in the profession," they responded.

Actually, Harry put it this way, "That is a *Judenfrei* department except for one man who is a Unitarian." He meant there were no Jews, and on purpose. There was, in fact, one faculty member, John Baptist Wolf, who had a picture of himself in his office wearing a Nazi uniform, if you can believe that. He didn't stay too much longer after I got there.

It turned out that Franklin and Carman were a little behind the times because when I arrived two Jewish members of the department had already been hired, Burton Stein in South Asia and Indian history, and Josef Altholz in English history. But I did learn why Carman and Franklin felt that way.

Burt was appointed to the department to replace a notorious anti-Semite. This was done by Herbert Heaton, the chairman of the History Department, as a deliberate affront to this notorious anti-Semite, who had been a historian of the British Empire. Obviously, by hiring Burt, a Jew, who was also a historian of India, not the British in the British Empire, but the Indians, it was a double affront to this man. Heaton was a working-class Londoner who became an economic historian of note and was a decent human being.

As an aside, a few years later, when we were looking for an African

American historian, our top candidate was Allan Spear from the University of Chicago, who had just written a brilliant dissertation on black Chicago. When I went to pick up Allan at the airport, I jokingly cautioned him, knowing Allan was Jewish, that as far as everybody in the History Department was concerned, he should actually be Allan "Schpeer," somehow related to the Nazi Albert Speer, so that nobody should know that.

After I was appointed, the then-chairman of the department, Harold Deutsch, said to David Noble, "David, don't you think we have enough of them by now?" A few years later, when I felt more secure and at home and in power, I confronted Deutsch in the place where you usually confronted people, the men's room.

"Harold, what have you got against short people?"

"What do you mean, what have I got against short people?"

"Didn't you at one time ask David, 'Don't we have enough of them by now?'" He almost went in his pants. That was one of those confrontational things I had with him.

I taught most of my first and second years at the University of Minnesota in the Social Sciences program, where I had a wonderful group of colleagues. Art Naftalin had been in the program, but by the time I arrived he had become mayor of the city of Minneapolis. Andreas Papandreou, previously in the Social Sciences program, was leading the Greek socialist movement at the time, and he was there. It was a distinguished group of people that I was becoming a part of. But when I got there, the remnant of the program was very small because it was being eliminated.

The courses we taught were general education courses of an interdisciplinary nature. Work, culture, and society were the general themes, and I was hired there largely because I was doing work on labor history. Labor history at Minnesota had been taught previously in the Economics Department. As far as I know, the University of Minnesota Department of History was the first in the nation that offered labor history as an undergraduate and graduate field of study. In a way, I pioneered in that. This labor history emphasis coincided with an opportunity that came somewhat out of the blue. Just about as soon as I arrived in Minnesota I was drafted for a project that would change my life and my connection to the state. In my life of transitions, this was a big one.

The University's president, O. Meredith Wilson, had received a massive grant from the Ford Foundation for a study of the impact of education on immigrants in Minnesota. He decided to have the focus of the study be on the immigrant iron miners in northern Minnesota, where the concentration of immigrants and their children was at its densest in the early part of the twentieth century and into the middle part of the twentieth century. Wilson was clearly too busy to conduct the research himself, so he farmed it out to three of us in History: Timothy Smith, Clarke Chambers, and me. Chambers focused on the impact of social welfare agencies. Smith focused on the immigrants and public education, and I dived into the immigrant communities themselves, their labor and ethnicities.

What we encountered on the Iron Range was the imminent disappearance of a generation and its records, and the slipping away of an immigrant generation that still lived, worked, and thought in its native tongues, and that had been the creator of cultural, fraternal, and political institutions. It was a generation of immigrants largely from Eastern and Southern Europe for which there did not yet exist anywhere in the country any widespread institutions of documentary preservation of their records and history.

German, Irish, and Jewish historical societies of one kind or another existed. There were large repositories of those kinds of materials, but no one was collecting the work of the Finns or of the south Slavs, or of the Italians for that matter. Eventually, an archival collection was organized and, of course, the University of Minnesota now has a world-leading Immigration History Research Center, but it wouldn't have happened without this Iron Range project, and I credit Tim Smith with being committed to the collection process. But the center didn't truly get off the ground until Rudy Vecoli arrived from the University of Illinois and turned it into the national gem it is today.

Of course, when I first arrived in northern Minnesota I knew as much about the Iron Range as Iron Rangers know about the Lower East Side of New York, which is absolutely nothing. One of the people who was most helpful in giving me an orientation to the Range, to be sure with his own personal twist, was a young dentist in his early thirties who was just getting started in his career in politics up in Hibbing. His name was Rudolph G. Perpich. His friends called him Rudy. He had already been a member of the Hibbing School Board that began giving equal pay for equal work for women teachers. When I met him, he was set to run for the Minnesota Senate.

It turned out that Rudy and I had more things in common than we even knew. To be sure, he came from a Croatian family and I came from a Polish, Jewish family. His father, Anton, was an iron ore miner and my father was a garment worker. His father was an anticlerical radical, who was a Socialist and I think on the fringe of the Communist movement. My father was a nonreligious Jew deep into the Communist movement. His father was one of the participants in the organization of the Croatian Fraternal Union and the Croatian branch of the International Workers Order, which was, of course, the major organization in which my parents operated. Although we were from different parts of the country, New York and Minnesota, and he couldn't understand Yiddish, nor could I understand Croatian, it seemed that Rudy and I had some kind of chemistry that worked.

Anton recognized it, too, very quickly. In fact, when I first met the Perpiches, Rudy's youngest brother, Joseph, was just getting out of high school and coming to the University of Minnesota. His father told me that I should be like a surrogate father to him at the University. He never needed me, but that's all right. I said I would do so, and it showed the instant bond I had with the Perpiches, a bond that would intensify years later when Rudy became Minnesota's lieutenant governor and then governor.

My education on the Range was comprehensive. I got to know personalities and individuals in their local history. We wrote a very important series of essays, the three of us, but Timothy's essay and mine contradicted each other. He was an assimilationist, a kind of flag-waver for the absence of conflict. I would call him an enthusiast for conformity and uniformity. My paper highlighted the differences between ethnic groups such as the Finns and Slovenian immigrant miners. I argued for the value of differences and how major conflicts had a role to play in the formation of institutions and of attitudes on the Iron Range.

The final result of the project was a major conference sponsored by the University. It was chaired by University president Wilson, and every kind of American historian was invited to the conference. The Iron Range conference had a profound impact. The paper I wrote is constantly cited all over the place. It was never published because the Ford Foundation's regulations required that it be unpublished. We could have written a book, but the three of us could never get together on writing a book.

If I hadn't realized it from my own family's experience, the Iron Range project helped me to fully understand that an immigrant coming to the United States is truly performing a revolutionary act. He makes a break from his own tradition. He is, in fact, cutting the ties that kept him in his old village or town. This is rejecting ancestry, rejecting nationality, rejecting home, and, sometimes even, rejecting religion. It's quite dramatic.

Carrying oneself and one's possessions and one's family over three thousand miles of ocean and another two thousand miles of land is a tremendous, wrenching transformation of the individual. Now, what causes people to migrate emerges from a combination of forces: discontent with what existed in their native land and a revolution of rising expectations. But a good part of it is a kind of image of what is hoped to be gained in America, the image of American promise, so to speak. It still exists today for our new immigrants.

Back when my parents came here, the American promise was actually far from being the American performance for these immigrants. It was hard, not only to become adjusted to American realities, to the New World, to the place where no one understood what these people were talking about. But, more important, those immigrants found themselves economically, at least, on the lowest rung of the ladder, being extremely exploited, doing the dirtiest work for the lowest wages, being first to be fired and the last to be hired. That was the Iron Range experience. And, if immigrants of all kinds went to farms, they found that the homestead tradition might have been fine in the promotional literature the railroads and steamship companies might have sent them, but, in reality, the only land that was left for them for homesteading purposes was scrubland, rocky land, land that could not produce.

Obviously, these immigrants would be discontented and dissatisfied, and this would lead them to question the realities of the American promise. Some would seek to reshape the performance into the promise. Others would seek a radical transformation. And, obviously, the discontent would lead to some kind of individual or social action. Insofar as this was the experience of the immigrant, it's understandable that a large proportion of them were going to become active in dissident politics, radical politics, radical movements like Anton and my father did.[1]

What this Iron Range experience did, what these realizations about the immigrant experience did, was, more or less, transform my academic interests and me. I became a Minnesota historian and, within a couple of years, I became known as the state's historian, which is pretty funny because two years earlier I thought Minnesota was no different from the other Ms in the nation: Michigan, Montana, Missouri. I mean, what's the difference? And my parents still didn't get that Minnesota was fairly safe. When my father heard I was coming to Minnesota, he asked, "Will you have to fight with the Indians?"

Social Sciences, Berzerk-ley, and an Absent Moos

I came into the University of Minnesota Social Sciences program at a time of confusing and almost debilitating transition. In 1961 sociologist David "Dan" Cooperman was chairing it. It had, at that point, lost just about every one of its tenured faculty members. In that transitional period, from 1961 to 1968, I taught one or two courses a year in the program, but most of my teaching responsibility had moved into the History Department as I hoped and preferred. I found the Social Sciences program, when I first came into it, both an exciting and a depressing place. It was exciting in its interdisciplinary concept. Its execution was horrible.

It was done largely by untrained graduate students who were taken on to support their graduate work and who were as interested in developing a course as one would expect. That is, not at all. The graduate student is busy trying to complete his own or her own—mostly then it was his—graduate work. Like I said, the idea was great. The execution was awful.

As can be expected, the University formed a big task force to look into the future of the social sciences and humanities interdisciplinary programs. I'm not a big fan of task forces, so I happily went off to be-

---

1. [Some of this material was developed from an interview of Professor Berman by student reporter Garrison Keillor on the campus radio station, KUOM, on July 16, 1966.—J.W.]

come a visitor at the University of California, Berkeley in 1967–68. In many ways, what a traumatic year it was.

My invitation to Berkeley came as a result of Larry Levine going on his sabbatical leave. Larry was an old friend from City College and Columbia days. They asked him to recommend someone, and he recommended me. There was lots of support for me among Berkeley's pretty remarkable history faculty. Among them was Leon Litwack, who was previously at the University of Wisconsin before he went on to Berkeley. When he was at Wisconsin he was a labor historian. When he went to Berkeley, he became a historian of African American culture. That's how people change, and Leon's work went on to win a National Book Award and a Pulitzer Prize. Hans Rosenberg, who was my colleague at Brooklyn College and then a German history scholar at Cal, confirmed that I was a good teacher. They were very much interested in my coming out there because of the seminar I could offer in labor radicalism in American society, which no one had ever given there.

Fortuitously, a professor of urban planning was going on leave to London and he had a beautiful home on El Dorado Street, in the foothills of the mountains there, just below where the great slavery and Reconstruction historian Ken Stampp lived, and the urban planning guy was willing to rent it to me. It was a big, beautiful house and it was comparable to my house near the Mississippi River in Minneapolis, so I wasn't giving up anything. I was able to rent our Seabury Avenue house to a visiting professor coming to Minnesota, so it was a very easy exchange going to Berkeley. We took a cross-country car trip to Berkeley, Betty, my then three kids—Ruth Steve, and Shelly—and me. The car was loaded by my graduate students, who did a good job tying things on the roof. That's what graduate students are good for sometimes. I was in Berkeley from the beginning of August 1967 until the middle of September of 1968, and it was a full year, to be sure.

When I first arrived there, I was warmly greeted and was immediately brought into a friendly milieu, both in terms of academic interests and in terms of political concerns and activities. Most of my colleagues were, like me, against the Vietnam War and hostile to the 1968 presidential candidacy of Hubert Humphrey of Minnesota. Most were working for Eugene McCarthy, the *other* Minnesota senator, or Bobby Kennedy. I was for McCarthy.

There was also a very active involvement on the part of the faculty in the emerging Black Power movement, which had the effect of dividing some of my faculty colleagues. Particularly the issues around Israel divided many of them. Nathan Glazer, who was not in the History Department, but in the Sociology Department at Berkeley, was an acquaintance of mine. We worked together in 1954 with my mentor, Salo Baron, on the Jewish Tercentenary project, marking the three-hundredth anniversary of the arrival of Jews in the United States. Glazer became increasingly hostile to the academic political activities of the left and became more and more inclined to move in a position of hostility and opposition to the antiwar movement, the Black Power movement, and the peace movement. He believed, as did others like him, that the movement was rejecting the whole concept of egalitarianism, equal opportunity, and the right of people to rise by their own merits.

Fundamentally, also, it was moving inexorably into a hostile mode toward Israel, which had succeeded in defeating the combined Arab forces in the 1967 Six-Day War, and was not the powerless victim but the powerful victor. This brought tension among some of my friends and colleagues, which, toward the end of my stay there, led to some social difficulties. You couldn't have a party with some people there when other people were there. It was that kind of thing. That was one aspect of being in Berkeley.

Then there was teaching. I taught the labor history seminar for graduate students and it was an extraordinary group, a handful of whom went on to become scholars in their own right. We became a close-knit group. We not only met at the seminar but also went out for beer and had dinner together. It was an experience like none I'd had at Minnesota. My graduate students at Minnesota were much more diverse in their thinking and separate from each other. To offer a seminar in labor and radical history in Berkeley in this turbulent year of 1967–68 was a magnificent experience. The historiographical debates turned into discussions of daily tactics.

For my undergraduate teaching, I did a survey U.S. history course with Southern historian Charlie Sellers and Leon Litwack. We developed a multimedia course. In those days multimedia meant three slide projectors. We had three slide projectors with a lot of sound, which was music Litwack put together. It was an exciting course experience, so much so that when I came back to Minnesota I made sure to invite Litwack to try it out on our students. It didn't go over too well here. Apparently, the cultural avant-gardism of the Berkeley students had not yet penetrated into the ranks of the Minnesota students.

All in all, I guess the Berkeley students were somewhere between my New York City College/Brooklyn College students and my Minnesota students. My City College students were characterized by my experience that when I walked into a classroom and said, "Good morning!" they'd shout out, "Yeah, what's so good about it?" My Minnesota students, when I'd say, "Good morning!" they'd write it into their notebooks. The Berkeley students were somewhere in between. They weren't quite sure whether to challenge me or to write it into their notebooks. They weren't quite as bold and as combative as the New York students, but they were certainly not as reticent and as docile in copying everything into notebooks as my students at Minnesota. In terms of the quality of the students, I could see very little difference.

As I said, these were turbulent times, and I inadvertently got caught right in the middle of them. One day I was returning from lunch, going back to Dwinelle Hall from Telegraph Avenue, and I ran into a group of picketers of one kind or another. Peter Camejo, the Trotskyist leader, who later ran for president of the United States on the Socialist Workers Party ticket, was there. He pointed at me and said, "There's a police spy!" Me, a police spy?

They started coming at me until one of the protestors yelled, "No, it's Professor Berman. He teaches labor history. He's one of us." I was able to get out.

Another interesting event occurred during my undergraduate course with Litwack and Sellers when we decided to show the film *Birth of a Nation,* the pro–Ku Klux Klan movie from 1915. *Birth of a Nation* had not been widely released at that time, but we found an archival copy of it and presented it. We showed it at night so there would be a bigger audience.

To our chagrin, walking into the auditorium to watch the film was a contingent of Black Panthers led by Bobby Seale, one of the Panthers' founders. We were concerned that there would be some kind of an upheaval. But, no, they sat through the film quietly, they hooted on occasion, and after the film was over they joined in the discussion and the conversation, which was, to some extent, illuminating and not as heated as I thought it would be.

Some of the extracurricular activities we were engaged in went beyond the political. Leon Litwack and a few others of my colleagues were avid football fans, as am I. We had season tickets to the Golden Bears, the University of California football team (I can't confuse them with the Golden Gophers). We went religiously to every home game and had a great time. On Sundays, it was football too. We went out for dim sum in San Francisco and then went to 49ers games.

I also had an opportunity to revisit my old New York love affair with the New York Giants, now the San Francisco Giants. I'd go out to Candlestick Park with my son, Steve. My father visited us once, and we'd boo the Giants because they left our beloved New York only ten years earlier. But how could I boo them when there was Willie Mays playing in the outfield? I guess we went there to boo *and* cheer.

At the end of my stay in Berkeley, I was given a party and a lot of my colleagues felt very sorry for me that I was going from this pinnacle of academic and climatological excellence back to the hellhole of the Siberian Midwest and Minnesota. When they asked me whether I'd be interested in staying at Berkeley, I had no idea whether this was a serious inquiry or not. My response was, "No, I have too many commitments to Minnesota and have too much going for me there." They couldn't understand that at all. I suspect that had I said, "Yes, I'm interested in staying," they probably would have found a way to keep me there, but I said, no, I want to go back. My last days there were almost like a wake. Everybody came to sit shiva for me. It was really pitiful.

When I told my Berkeley colleagues I had too much going for me in Minnesota, I meant it. As my visitorship ended, I received a phone call from Lloyd Lofquist, who was then associate dean of the University of Minnesota's College of Liberal Arts. That task force looking into the Social Sciences program had done its work, and then there was a search committee named to find a new director for Social Sciences. I was their top candidate and Lloyd asked me if I'd take over.

"What Social Sciences program?" I asked.

"You're right. It can be anything you want to make of it within the framework of interdisciplinary social sciences."

"Let me think about it."

To take over a program that is nonexistent is really, well, thank you for the honor, but what's the honor? That evening, I got a phone call from the dean of CLA, E. W. "Easy" Ziebarth. Lloyd apparently told Easy of my reaction, that to take over a shell that's about to disintegrate is not something I'd like to do. So, Easy said, "There are many opportunities, many things you can do. You'll have my backing."

The Social Sciences program was part of the general education setup that was very popular during the 1940s and '50s, following Columbia University and University of Chicago models. By the 1960s it was becoming obsolete, largely because of the growth of the emphasis on disciplines and the disciplinary control of undergraduate education. In effect, my role as the director of the Social Sciences program was to supervise its liquidation. But since I had experienced Berkeley and its academic and political turmoil, I wanted to somehow or other prevent that from happening at the U. I saw the program as a way in which we could change the curriculum and make it more relevant to the needs of students of the latter half of the twentieth century.

Remember to put this in the time frame. This was a time of massive upheaval in the halls of academia, massive upheaval in the nation itself. This was a period of radical if not revolutionary reevaluation of the role of higher education in our society. Perhaps it was too frantic and frenetic a period—I agree it was—but it called for some sense of experimentation and renewal.

We had a very powerful and inclusive advisory committee of high-ranking faculty, with people from the College of Agriculture, from Business Administration, and from the Institute of Technology creating new courses and new approaches. Some of them were crazy, touchy-feely kinds that were a symptom of the times. But we tried everything. If 5 percent would work, be integrated into the curriculum, and become successful, that would be a good track record. Some people would look at the other 95 percent that didn't work and say, "It's a waste of time, waste of money." No, it wasn't a waste of money because almost everybody was doing it as overload. It was the cheapest program we ever had.

If you look at the evolution of new courses, new curriculum, new departments, and new programs from about 1968 to 1974, sure, some failed and some succeeded, but all came through the Social Sciences program, which made it possible for me to work with other like-minded faculty members to pioneer in the creation of new areas of intellectual inquiry. It was through the Social Sciences program that we were able to start an Urban Studies program. Never before at Minnesota had we had one. John Borchert, a distinguished geographer, and I cofounded the Urban Studies curriculum development. Experimental courses were offered in women's studies, which led to the formation of the Women's Studies Department. We had a role, too, in the establishment of the African and African American Studies Department, but it was student anger and protest that pushed its creation forward in a dramatic way.

This was the political backdrop to it all. In the fall of 1968, when I returned from Berkeley, the explosion of student New Left activism took on the form of teach-ins and protest strikes. I was able, together with my colleague Burnham Terrell of the Philosophy Department, who was then the director of the Honors Division of the College of Liberal Arts, to use the Social Sciences program as a means of creating ad hoc courses that would take the place of regular courses during strike times. The courses were a bit, I guess you could say, avant-garde, in that they were courses in which the instructors were people from the University community and from the black community. They were joint courses taught by two groups of people. Academic Vice President William Shepherd said to me that I was "socializing" protest by doing these things. Whether I was socializing protest or not, I was able to move with the New Left in trying to channel its activities on campus in a more creative and constructive way.

But things were changing. This was a period of history in the academic world when a university wasn't a university unless it was taken over by students. The black students at our university were becoming increasingly restive under conditions on campus. In early 1968 through early 1969, a group of activist black students began agitating for the development of a department of African and African American studies. At the same time, the dean of the College of Liberal Arts asked me to look into the possibility of developing a graduate program in comparative race and ethnicity. This was built upon the strength we had in developing immigrant archives and the Immigrant History Research Center, and our integrating race into a discussion of academic packages that would have dealt with the issue.

It was in the midst of our deliberations—discussions more than deliberations because I don't think we got very far in deliberations—that the University of Minnesota's black students demanded, and rightly so, some kind of curriculum access. What they wanted, of course, was a Black studies department, which was part of the national pressure going on. Cornell, in particular, was exploding, among other campuses.

Whenever our students came to the powers that be, that is to say to the dean or the president, they'd hear, "We have a committee working on it."

Malcolm Moos was a political scientist and former journalist who had been President Dwight David Eisenhower's speechwriter. He was responsible for warning against—and creating the term—the "military-industrial complex" in Eisenhower's farewell speech. But as University president, Moos turned out to be a disappointment.

To be sure, he reflected the values of a liberal academic institution, continuing the open tradition that O. Meredith Wilson had fostered, but Moos came into the presidency at a time when the political and economic crisis began to play an increasingly erosive role at the University of Minnesota, and he was unable or unwilling to confront it.

It all came to a head in January 1969, when a group of black students asked for a meeting with President Moos. They had that meeting in his Morrill Hall office and took him hostage when he refused to immediately establish a department of African and African American studies. In fact, he argued with them, saying that I chaired a committee that was looking into that, which wasn't quite true. My committee was looking into a graduate program in comparative ethnic and racial history, but I think there was enough truth to it to just be credible.

I had a call to my office that afternoon from President Moos, who seemed a bit harassed and a bit breathless, and he asked me if I would quickly come over to his office to talk to some students who had an interest in what my committee was doing. He didn't tell me that he was under siege. That I learned when I first got there, when I walked to the president's office and saw the University Police surrounding it. They said, "Professor Berman, you go right in," and they were keeping everybody else out.

I went in and, of course, Moos introduced them. I knew most of them—Anna Stanley, Rosemary Freeman, and Horace Huntley, who went on to become an African American history professor at the University of

Alabama at Birmingham. Moos said, "Oh, here's Professor Berman. He will tell us exactly what's going on." And I'm thinking, "What the hell am I getting myself into here?"

I thought I'd try to be rational. I said, "Look, a black studies department is a desirable outcome down the road a piece. We have no pool of academic talent to mount such a department. The focus on graduate education is really the way to go because then we will get a pool of talent to move into a department." That made no impression whatsoever. I thought it was rational. They thought it was rationalization.

I presented what the committee had been working on and what our thinking was on how this would inevitably lead to programs in African and African American studies. But I said that the committee wasn't yet ready to report its findings, and academic planning takes a little bit longer than a month or so, and that we were exploring courses in comparative race and ethnicity. Nobody was buying any of it, especially courses in comparative race. Rosemary Freeman interrupted and said, "We're not interested in comparing nothing with nothing."

That epitomized the mood of the gathering there. They occupied the building and closed it. But not before President Moos excused himself and said he had to go to the bathroom and they let him go. But he never came back. He just upped and left, so there I was, the hostage now who was under control of the black students. At this point, they and their Students for a Democratic Society supporters had taken over the entire administration building, Morrill Hall, from top to bottom. All the workers in the building had been dismissed, asked to leave, and the building was occupied by the students.

Then Burnham Terrell, my partner in crime in many activities, was also quickly called to come to Morrill Hall to talk to the students. Vice President of Administration Don Smith was also brought in, as was Jim Reeves, a black staff member of the Student Affairs Office. The four of us, with some community people assisting, constituted a floating group of negotiators.

We negotiated through the night, and around eleven o'clock I had done as much as I could and said I was going to go home, and the students let me go home. I got a meal and went to sleep. At two in the morning, the phone rang. It was Don Smith, who said it had come to a crisis and we had to solve the situation now.

So I got into the car and ran down to Morrill Hall and we came to an agreement. We were able to get the students to agree that we couldn't immediately create a department. That was an academic exercise, it took time, but we would move toward the development of a program in African and African American studies that would within the next year or so offer meaningful courses. The reason I was able to make that decision was that we knew a number of such courses were already being offered in various departments, and there were some in the pipeline that were about to be presented. Fred Lukermann, who was assistant vice president of academic affairs, had been working for the establishment of what later came to be known as the Martin Luther King Fund, a scholarship fund for needy students, primarily black, but others as well. So we included that in our agreement. They wanted some money for a conference, and we were able to come up with some money for a conference. And that was essentially the package deal that we came up with.

In these final negotiations, Don Smith represented the administration. President Moos was at Eastcliff, the official residence of University presidents, and we didn't know what he was doing there. In order to get full agreement we needed the president to go along with it. So Don Smith took the agreement, and now it was three or four in the morning, and he went to Eastcliff to get the president's approval.

Terrell, Reeves, Smith, and I then went back to the students and said we had an agreement. As we left the building, the press was going crazy bananas, wanting to know what we agreed to. We said that what we agreed to would come out in a statement to the Faculty Senate and we are not going to release it until the Faculty Senate got it. We presented it to the Senate and we were attacked by the academic conservatives. Fortunately, the majority of the Senate saw that our position was better than our attackers', and they confirmed the agreement. The siege was over.

I saw one thing there that I've been using in discussions with media people ever since, and that's how the media sometimes manipulates the news. The impression that the Twin Cities received or, for that matter, that the nation received of the black occupation of Morrill Hall was that it was chaotic and destructive. It was not. Yes, it was chaotic, but, no, it was not destructive.

Why did they get the impression that it was destructive? A television news team from one of the local television networks, a news reporter, who later went on to become a state official, didn't like the visuals they were getting so they came into the basement of Morrill Hall, and started taking things off desks, and throwing them all over the place, and taking pictures of it. I happened to pass by when it happened and shouted at them, "Get the fuck out of here."

Nonetheless, that evening on the news came this picture of this massive destruction. It turns out that afterward, when they totaled up the damage, it came to under $10,000. I'm not condoning $10,000 worth of damage, but I'm wondering how much of that damage was done by the television news teams and how much by the students.

In the end, the occupation led to the establishment of the Black Studies program. Similarly, when the pressures came on for Indian studies and for Chicano studies, it was all done again through the Social Sciences program, and without the same trauma. We staffed it. The secretary we had in the program was the secretary for all of these things. It was through the associate dean's office and my office that we were able to work out the arrangements. My long-term commitment to cultural autonomy came to life amid all of this on-campus revolution.

4 The Making of Hubert Humphrey

My first brush with Minnesota politics came in the 1961 mayoral campaign in Minneapolis. In a sense, this is where I made my first connection with the legacy of Hubert Humphrey.

The election was actually held in June, just as Betty and I were moving from Michigan State. I didn't know anybody, I didn't know anything, but all my University acquaintances were backing this nice political scientist by the name of Arthur Naftalin. In order to be mayor of Minneapolis he had to beat out another progressive candidate who was from the labor movement, David Roe.

Dave Roe was from the building trades. I was told immediately by my colleagues, whom I trusted, that those were right-wingers. The building trades were right wing. Coming from a Congress of Industrial Organizations Communist Party tradition, I could believe that. I'd learn later that the building trades were different in the Twin Cities from New York. But, then, it was obvious. I would support Art Naftalin. He was an academic and Jewish. Two good things. I actually didn't know then that he was on Hubert Humphrey's staff during Humphrey's years as Minneapolis mayor. And that's where my links to Humphrey and my understanding of the Democratic-Farmer-Labor Party would begin.

It wasn't only by Naftalin's candidacy, but by a truly Minnesota phenomenon, that I was immediately brought into DFL culture. It was the "bean feed," which was the most significant form of fund-raising in the DFL Party. It was like it sounds it is. You ate beans. You mingled. You contributed a little bit of money. It was not your thousand-dollar-a-plate dinner, that's for sure.

The most significant bean feed I attended in my first years in Minnesota was at the State Fairgrounds at which President John Kennedy was the main speaker. Go to a fair with the president as the main speaker? In New York I couldn't do that. I didn't have a million dollars to go to a dinner. In Minnesota all you needed was five bucks to go to a bean feed with the president of the United States. I went with more than five bucks because some of my colleagues were involved in DFL politics, so they got me on the platform. Here I was in my second year in Minnesota, and there I was fifty feet from John Kennedy and forty-five feet from Hubert Humphrey. In New York it would have taken me a lifetime to get within two blocks of those guys. So I said, hey, this Minnesota is an interesting place.

Then there was the election campaign in 1962 for governor. When I first came to Minnesota, the governor was Elmer Andersen, whom I later got to know and became very friendly with when he was a member of the University of Minnesota's Board of Regents. Yes, I know it's hard to believe, but we became friends even though he was a Republican.

Andersen was running for reelection and the DFL candidate was Karl Rolvaag. Karl Rolvaag had a long party history, was a party chair, had been an activist. He was the son of Ole Rolvaag, the great Norwegian American novelist, who was a professor of Norwegian language and literature at St. Olaf College. Karl was a respected individual, so obviously I was going to support the DFL candidate, not some Republican. I must admit, and I did confess to Elmer Andersen later in life, that one of my first political acts in Minnesota was to draft a slogan that was used by the Rolvaag campaign. The slogan, which became very popular, was put on bumper stickers. It was "Back to Glue in '62."

You have to be a Minnesotan to understand that slogan. Elmer was the president of H. B. Fuller, which is still an adhesives and glue company. So I figured it was "Back to Glue in '62" if he won again. He lost after a recount by ninety-one votes, the first great Minnesota recount before the 2008 Al Franken–Norm Coleman U.S. Senate recount. By the way, when I told Elmer Andersen about the glue slogan some years later, his reaction was, "And I thought you were my good friend." I said, "Yes, I am, but that's now and not then."

So, almost immediately upon coming to Minnesota I got involved in these things and this merged nicely with my Iron Range work to make me an instant Minnesotan. But it was national politics that mattered to me more. And this is really where my relationship with Hubert developed.

By 1964–65 it was clear to a number of us that the Vietnam adventure we were getting into was dangerous and maybe even a disaster. In '64 I was sent by the University of Minnesota to Osmani University in Hyderabad, India, to set up an American history/American studies program for that area. I actually missed the U.S. presidential election of 1964 because I was in Hyderabad. I was there for three months, from September through December, which was during the buildup that was taking place not that far from India in Southeast Asia. I came back from India convinced that this was the wrong thing to do.

Burt Stein, who was our East Asian historian, Romeyn Taylor, our Chinese historian, and Josef Altholz, our English history scholar, and I went to visit Congressman Donald Fraser, who was on the House Foreign Affairs Committee. We spoke with Don about the situation in Southeast Asia, and he also had become very uncomfortable with the situation. When we presented our facts, he became an active opponent to our escalation in Vietnam.

The basis of my opposition was very practical. It was absolutely the case that we were siding with the wrong forces, the reactionary forces, the Catholic forces that were trying to impose Catholicism in a Buddhist country, that we were supporting a colonialist policy that was already repudiated in the rest of the world, and that it was doomed to fail. That was essentially my position at the time. At best, this was a civil war in which we had no reason to get involved. At worst, we were getting involved with the wrong people.

The DFL situation was increasingly becoming difficult, particularly when Humphrey became a major possibility to become Lyndon Johnson's vice presidential running mate in 1964. Johnson had adopted not only the Kennedy policies of social reform, social change, the Great Society, and the War on Poverty but also Kennedy's Cold War policies, which included escalation of the war in Vietnam.

It was at this point that some critical distance began to develop between those of us who argued against the Vietnam War and those who supported Humphrey, who was now a part of the Johnson wing of the Democratic Party. I didn't really know Hubert Humphrey at all then. I had met him a number of times, seen him at a bean feed or two, and, if you remember, had listened to his speech to eliminate my New York accent, which was a losing battle. It wasn't until after he lost his election for the presidency in 1968 that I got to know him very well.

But before then I was in Berkeley as a visiting professor during much of the 1968 presidential campaign, and like most of my Cal colleagues I was an active supporter of Eugene McCarthy, the longtime U.S. congressman and the other senator from Minnesota. Whoever was the Democratic nominee, we had to beat Richard Nixon. Sometime in late 1967 or early 1968, Art Naftalin came to Berkeley and looked me up. He asked me if I wouldn't want to join the Humphrey campaign staff and, maybe, even the White House staff, if he were elected. I guess Art was shocked when I told him what my positions were.

I threw up my hands and said, "I'm backing Gene McCarthy, and I'm in the antiwar movement, and you want me to back a warmonger?" I meant Humphrey the warmonger.

Art replied, "Take it easy. Don't get excited. I know you've been infected by the Berkeley bug. Just think about it for a while. Do you want Nixon?"

I thought about it for a while and then Art said, "Look, when you get back to Minnesota, there will still be plenty of time to think this over."

This was a paid campaign position he was offering and I would have had to take a leave from teaching and leave Berkeley immediately. Besides, I was very actively involved in California trying to mobilize the support for McCarthy for the primary against his main opponent, Robert Kennedy.

I was never a big fan of Bobby Kennedy. I looked upon him as an opportunist, a Johnny-come-lately, and when they were trying to build him up as a kind of man of the people, I thought, "Man of the people, my ass." He worked for Wisconsin senator Joe McCarthy's Permanent Subcommittee on Investigations, harassing and bullying progressive people, and all of a sudden he becomes Cesar Chavez's best friend and a lover of farmworkers? I didn't buy that for one minute. Of course, I felt sorry for him and his family when he was assassinated. But I was not going to support him over Gene McCarthy.

When I got back to Minnesota, Art put me in touch with Hubert Humphrey. It was now in the heat of the full presidential campaign. After a half hour or an hour of conversation with Humphrey, I came away with the impression that, despite our obvious differences on Vietnam, I'd better back this man or feel sorry for the rest of my life. I agreed to Art's request and I supported Humphrey. I lost a lot of my friends because of it.

Looking back, I laugh now that I ever questioned Humphrey's potential and motivations. He was the most influential Minnesota politician of the twentieth century and, perhaps, ever. That's why it's important to put his lifetime of accomplishments in perspective.

First, let's address his role in the birth of the Democratic-Farmer-Labor Party, which remains unique in the nation to this day.[1] Now, I don't want to rain on anyone's parade, but my graduate students' research years ago destroyed the mythology that Humphrey was the force behind the merger of the Democratic and Farmer-Labor Parties in 1944. First of all, Humphrey was thirty-three years old when the DFL was formed. I don't know too many thirty-three-year-olds who play a critical leading role in any political movement. He was also then a graduate student. This is the man who was going to forge a merger of two political parties in the 1940s? No way.

Don't get me wrong. Hubert played a role in the merger. He was secretary of what was called the Unity Convention and, as such, played a significant role, but the merger of the Farmer-Labor Party and the Democratic Party is more interesting than what we know in conventional wisdom or more than the result of Hubert's inspirational personality. To me, the architects of the merger were, in fact, not Minnesotans at all. The architects of the merger were in Washington and in New York. In Washington, the White House. In New York, Twelfth Street. Those of you who don't know what the designation of Twelfth Street means, let me tell you. It was the headquarters of the American Communist Party. This was an architected combination that found its way to Minnesota and in Minnesota. The genesis of all of this goes way back to August 8, 1934, or ten years before the merger.

---

1. [Much of this material about Humphrey's role in the DFL and in various political conventions is adapted from remarks Berman made at Minneapolis City Hall on May 27, 2011, on the one hundredth anniversary of Humphrey's birth and from appearances on the Twin Cities PBS show *Almanac* on July 14, 2000; August 11, 2000; and August 18, 2000.—J.W.]

Why do I say that? Very simply, the White House was concerned about the electoral votes for Minnesota in the 1936 presidential election. President Franklin Delano Roosevelt was in Rochester, Minnesota, to honor the Mayo brothers who started the Mayo Clinic. But he found time during the day, without any advisers, without any secretaries, to meet with Governor Floyd Olson, and what did they talk about? They spoke about the Minneapolis Truckers' Strike, which was still ongoing, very ugly, and deadly.

To be sure, they came to an agreement on the challenges of that strike, which ended just a couple of weeks later. But I believe the most important agreement they came to was a political alliance. Olson and Roosevelt were acquaintances, having served as governors together for almost two years. The arrangement they came to was a very simple one. It was that the Farmer-Labor Party in Minnesota, particularly under Olson's leadership, would do its best to prevent any kind of third-party challenge from the left of the Roosevelt election effort in 1936. In turn, FDR wouldn't endorse any Democratic gubernatorial candidate against Floyd Olson in his 1934 reelection, and the Democrats wouldn't even run anyone against any Farmer-Labor gubernatorial candidate in 1936. Those were the days when governors ran every two years. One other part of the deal: FDR would work so that the Democrats wouldn't run anyone against Floyd Olson if he ran for the U.S. Senate in 1936.

So it was a significant political arrangement that served the needs of both parties very, very well. In fact, by 1935 the Democratic Party and the New Dealers were moving closer to the position of Floyd Olson and the Farmer-Laborites. The heir to this FDR–Floyd Olson deal was Elmer Benson. As agreed to by FDR and Olson, Benson would run as the DFL candidate for governor in 1936 without any Democratic opposition and actually did go on to beat the Republican in a landslide. The point is that the activity in advance of and around the 1936 Democratic National Convention and the election laid the foundation for the end of the third-party movement in Minnesota.

This mutual aid relationship picked up even more in 1938, when Republicans made a remarkable comeback in Congress, gaining many seats. It reached a point where the White House political people were concerned that Roosevelt's reelection in 1940 could be jeopardized if Minnesota's electoral votes weren't delivered for FDR. They felt that the way this could be accomplished would be to unify the Farmer-Labor Party and the Democratic Party, to merge them.

Remember that the Democratic Party in Minnesota at that time was essentially a patronage party that consisted largely of the Catholic constituents in St. Paul and in St. Cloud. And the Farmer-Labor Party then was really dominated by the Popular Front. The Popular Front was a coalition of forces that worked from the left of center on issues and was allied with the American Communist Party.

Now the Communists come to this merger very simply, and that was the fear that Roosevelt's defeat in 1944 would jeopardize the World War II effort, and in 1943 and 1944 the Communists were even more patriotic than any Americans. Of course, their concern was the security of the Soviet Union. Therefore, in Washington and in New York there was this joint feeling that Minnesota needed a single progressive party that would guarantee Roosevelt would be reelected in 1944. This, to me, was the motivation of the Democratic-Farmer-Labor merger. By the way, Roosevelt won Minnesota by five-and-a-half percentage points, two points less than he won the rest of the country. But, by '44 the Democratic-Farmer-Labor Party became one. Hubert was there, but he wasn't the primary force driving the merger. Let's get that clear for history.

Four years later it's 1948. Harry Truman is the unelected president of the United States, having taken office after Franklin Roosevelt died, and the Democrats are in turmoil. There's civil rights, there's the Cold War and our relationship with the Soviet Union, and then there's the Red Scare going on, all at the same time. And Truman is trying to unify all that. Frankly, he's trying to survive.

By '48 Humphrey had truly emerged as the voice and face of the DFL and progressive politics in Minnesota. He was moving from the Minneapolis mayor role to a candidate for the U.S. Senate. By then, as mayor, one of his trademark accomplishments was fighting anti-Semitism in Minneapolis. His activism on that front, which set him up for national prominence, all seemingly started with a 1946 article written by journalist and commentator Carey McWilliams titled, "Minneapolis: The Curious Twin." It appeared in the journal *Common Ground,* which was a leader in promoting cultural pluralism.

Most of us are familiar with one sentence of the article—one sentence alone is the only one that matters—and that's the assertion that

Minneapolis had become "the capitol [sic] of anti-Semitism in the United States." Anti-Semitism had long been part of Minnesota's statewide DNA, but McWilliams's article specifically exposed the distinction between Minneapolis and St. Paul and their respective relationships to their Jewish communities.

The evidence that Minneapolis was the capital of anti-Semitism was pretty thorough. On the social side, there was no intermingling. The Jewish community was, in fact, isolated. There was, for example, a prohibition against Jews being in the Automobile Club. What, Jews can't drive? We could drive. The more difficult question was the question of economic integration. Jews were kept out of major occupations and jobs throughout the city, jobs that were open to Jews elsewhere.

One example: first-generation Jews, the children of immigrants, were able to move out of their proletarian status by going to the University of Minnesota, and most who went to the University went on to become teachers because that was the easiest way out of poverty. Consequently, the first breakthrough—social and economic breakthroughs—that we saw in the children of immigrants was the move by Jews into public education systems around the country. Even in Minnesota we found Jewish teachers in outlying school districts throughout the state, but not in Minneapolis. McWilliams also wrote about the hostility of Evangelicals and Catholics against Jews. That's what I'd call clerical anti-Semitism, and it was prevalent throughout the city. There was a radio evangelist named Luke Rader, who beamed his anti-Semitism across the nation from a tabernacle on Lake Street.

Why? Why was Minneapolis this way? And why was St. Paul different? Let's examine what McWilliams said. He wrote that the difference between Minneapolis and St. Paul was twofold. St. Paul was an older city, settled before we were even a state. Some of the first settlers were Jewish merchants. St. Paul right from the start was a very diverse population. There were, to be sure, large numbers of Germans—Catholic and Lutheran Germans. There were Irish Catholics and a wide range of Anglos, including the traditional New Englanders who settled in the early years of Minnesota's existence. This population mix led to an acceptance of Jews as an integral part of the St. Paul community.

Minneapolis, on the other hand, was a newer city, formed in the 1870s and '80s as the result of flour milling. Pillsbury's Best was all over the world. Washburn-Crosby, what we now know as General Mills, was all over the world. The mills were run by Anglos, but the overwhelming new populations of the city of Minneapolis were Scandinavians, Norwegians and Swedes. In Minneapolis the only others besides the Scandinavians were the Jews. There were very few blacks. Hardly any Irish Catholics, hardly any German Catholics. Every new community has an "other." There is us and them. And for the Scandinavians—not all of them, but most—there was no "other" but the Jews. In St. Paul the Jews were among the many "others," and so there was less hostility and anti-Semitism.

As Jews settled on the North Side of Minneapolis, there was a feeling among Scandinavians that their culture was under attack. The Jews looked different. They spoke Yiddish, a language that no one could understand, not even Germans. This hostility was great, and was not overcome until many years later.

This leads to the most egregious manifestation of political anti-Semitism in Minnesota history and that's during the race for Minnesota's governor in 1938. This, too, will lay the groundwork for Humphrey's battle against anti-Semitism eight years later. In my view, this '38 campaign is one we should never forget. That's why I first wrote about this in 1976 and regularly lectured about it.

The context can inform us today. Remember, like the rest of the nation, Minnesota experienced major economic and social dislocations as a consequence of the Great Depression. Accompanying massive unemployment in the urban areas was sharpened distress in the rural areas. Although predictions of social revolution proved groundless, political upheaval occurred.

The election of Floyd B. Olson, the Farmer-Labor candidate for governor in 1930, signaled the beginnings of a political and social change that was unanticipated by the wielders of power in the state. Since the Civil War, Republican domination of state politics had been the rule despite recurring protest movements: Grangers, Populists, Nonpartisan Leaguers, and Farmer-Laborites. The Democratic Party remained its insignificant patronage-dealing self, mainly centered in Catholic St. Paul and active only when Democratic presidents had jobs to distribute in the state.

Olson's election in 1930 and subsequent reelections in 1932 and 1934 changed this. For twenty-five years before that, the Twin Cities were dominated by a group of Republican bankers and businessmen organized in the Citizens Alliance, dedicated to preserving an "open shop" environment in the state. Through social and business contacts this political control covered the state from the Iron Range in the north to the grain-producing areas of the south and west.

This control was upset not only by the elections of 1930, 1932, and 1934 but also by what the Farmer-Labor victories promised. The open shop was destroyed in a series of massive and bloody strikes in 1934 and 1935 during which the Farmer-Labor administration used state power to aid and assist the strikers.

National pressure was applied through the Reconstruction Finance Corporation on the Twin Cities banks by the Roosevelt administration to compel recalcitrant, old-line openshoppers to bargain in good faith with their workers. To those accustomed to unrestricted use of power and access to the state instruments of power this overturning in fortunes constituted a major revolution.

Governor Olson was born and raised in North Minneapolis. His Norwegian father and Swedish mother were constantly fighting and young Floyd sought the companionship and warmth of his best friend's family, the Harrises, who were Jewish. North Minneapolis in the early twentieth century was the center of the Yiddish-speaking community, and young Floyd acted as the *Shabbos goy* for many of his Jewish neighbors. The *Shabbos goy* is the non-Jew who performs household tasks for observant Jews on Saturdays, the Sabbath. Lights candles, cooks, cleans. Olson also learned of the Jewish community's resistance to poverty and injustice.[2]

Throughout his political career Olson was better able to campaign in Yiddish than in either Swedish or Norwegian. It is not surprising, then, that he should surround himself with his Jewish friends when he became Hennepin County attorney late in 1920 and governor a little more than ten years later. This coincided with the coming to maturity of the second generation of Eastern European Jewish immigrants in Minnesota.

---

2. [Much of this section about the 1938 election is adapted from Hyman Berman, "Political Anti-Semitism in Minnesota during the Great Depression," *Jewish Social Studies* 38, no. 3/4, American Bicentennial I (Summer–Autumn 1976): 247–64.—J.W.]

A small but significant number of Jewish young people attended the University of Minnesota, completed Law or Journalism School, and embarked on political careers as staff people in the governor's office.

Additionally, Olson attracted a small number of more mature Jewish trade unionists and semiprofessionals who were placed in key patronage positions. Abe I. Harris became the editor of the *Minnesota Leader,* the mouthpiece for the Farmer-Labor Party and the official organ for the governor. Maurice Rose was appointed chauffeur and shared honors with George B. Leonard of being Olson's main drinking companion. Edward J. Pearlove was appointed state comptroller; Jean Spielman, state printer; Harry Fiterman, tax commissioner; and Roger Rutchick, assistant attorney general. For the first time in Minnesota history a significant number of Jews were appointed to state offices, and the consequent whispering campaign against Jewish dominance became a minor-key accompaniment to the antiradical rhetoric during Olson's reelection campaigns.

To enhance his national standing, Olson's advisers convinced him to run for the United States Senate in 1936. This threatened to split the Farmer-Labor Party wide open as several successors vied for the honor of succeeding to the governor's chair. When U.S. senator Thomas Schall, a Republican, was killed by a hit-and-run driver in Washington in December 1935, the internal differences within the party became open as the succession struggle began.

The group around Olson looked to Bank Commissioner Elmer A. Benson as Olson's successor and, to gain the edge for him, convinced the governor to appoint Benson to serve Schall's unexpired term, it being clearly understood that Benson would then step down from the Senate, would run for governor, and then Olson would run for the U.S. Senate the next year. Quite an arrangement, to be sure, but a progressive one.

The opposition to this plan within the DFL coalesced around Lieutenant Governor Hjalmar Petersen, who wanted Olson to resign as governor, enter the U.S. Senate, and be succeeded by Petersen in the governor's chair. Olson's appointment of Benson to the U.S. Senate soured Petersen, a highly ambitious and unprincipled politician who began a campaign of vilification against Olson, Benson, and their supporters by attacking the people around Governor Olson as, among other things, "Mexican Generals." The term "Mexican General" quickly became a code used to attack the Jewish advisers and officeholders surrounding Olson.

Despite Petersen's campaign against the "Mexican Generals" who, he claimed, tightly controlled the Farmer-Labor Party, the nominating convention proceeded as expected in endorsing Floyd B. Olson for the U.S. Senate seat and Elmer A. Benson for governor. To maintain harmony, Petersen was offered and accepted the nomination for railroad and warehouse commissioner.

But this shaky party harmony was shattered in the summer of 1936, when it became known to most insiders that Olson was dying of cancer. Olson's friends, among whom were Abe Harris and George Leonard, were determined to keep this fact a secret, but the scheme was revealed when, on August 12, ten days before Olson's death, Petersen wrote the governor demanding that, for reasons of health, he resign, convince Benson to run for election to the U.S. Senate, and allow Petersen to succeed to the governorship and run for election to that office in the fall. Petersen simply wouldn't give up.

Petersen's ambition destroyed whatever cordial relations still existed between him and the Olson group, and, after Olson's death, Benson reiterated his intention to run for governor and the Farmer-Labor Party's State Committee selected Ernest Lundeen to replace Olson as the party's U.S. Senate candidate.

The entire Farmer-Labor ticket was overwhelmingly elected in 1936. This was partially a result of the local expression of Franklin D. Roosevelt's landslide reelection victory and partially a result of statewide mourning over the death of "the Skipper," as Olson was nicknamed. Despite Republican efforts to depict Elmer Benson as a captive of communism and a tool of unscrupulous labor racketeers, Benson won with the largest majority given a gubernatorial candidate in Minnesota up to that time. The Farmer-Labor Party also gained control of the lower house of the legislature but not the state senate.

Before the oath of office had been administered to Elmer Benson, Hjalmar Petersen was in search of a constituency. As the Benson administration moved further to the left, so Petersen moved further in the opposite direction. I don't think Petersen consciously set out upon an anti-Semitic smear campaign against Benson, but through the early months of 1937 he repeated his "Mexican Generals" remarks without realizing that he was stirring up an undercurrent of political filth. Disgruntled applicants for jobs in the state administration wrote him applauding his attack and at first hinting at "Jew" control and later openly stating it.

For example, early in 1937, the superintendent of schools in Hastings, Minnesota, wrote Petersen, "The F-L Party is controlled by a few Jews who are shaking the state down for so much money." Another letter writer wrote, "Benson with his radical ideas, Jewish advisors and spend-thrift tactics ha[s] turned Mr. Average voter against him."

Petersen did not repudiate these charges, but rather consciously began making use of anti-Semitic innuendo in his public utterances. Increasingly Petersen alleged that Communist infiltrators had captured the Farmer-Labor governor and the party with the help of the "Mexican Generals."

Early in 1938 he announced that he would file for governor in the upcoming race without waiting for endorsement by the Farmer-Labor convention, thus challenging Benson to a primary election contest. When asked to name the "Mexican Generals" at a meeting on February 2, 1938, he answered, "Abe Harris, Art Jacobs, and Rutchick." Jacobs was secretary to the Speaker of the House. All three men were Jews.

Hjalmar Petersen began accumulating a following. Disgruntled job seekers, evangelical anti-Semites, and agrarian radicals with an anti-Semitic bent began flocking to Petersen's side. Funds to conduct his campaign were contributed by persons close to the United States Steel Corporation and the Northwestern Bank Corporation with the hope that Petersen would eliminate the radical Benson from Minnesota and national political life.

Despite massive Republican crossover votes in the Farmer-Labor primary, Benson squeaked through to victory with a sixteen-thousand-vote margin over Petersen out of a half million votes cast. Benson got the nomination and the preliminary round was over. The main event against the Republican challenger, a fellow named Harold E. Stassen, of South St. Paul, was on, and the Republicans picked up the anti-Semitic campaign where the Farmer-Labor opposition left off.

The chief architect of the Republican anti-Semitic campaign was Ray P. Chase of Anoka, Minnesota. Chase, with his brother, Roe, published and edited a local newspaper, the *Anoka Herald*. In 1916 he joined the staff of the state auditor, becoming state auditor himself in 1920. Chase was twice elected to this post, resigning in 1930 to run as Republican candidate for governor against Olson. In 1932 he was elected to the United States House of Representatives and, after two years of voting against every New Deal measure, was defeated in his bid for reelection in 1934. For the rest of his life, until his death in 1948, Chase devoted himself to unsuccessful attempts at gaining political office, but primarily to what he called "research" into corruption, mismanagement, and Communist activities in state government.

Ray Chase was no lunatic-fringe anti-Semite, but was in the mainstream of Old Guard Minnesota Republicanism for whom even Herbert Hoover was too far to the left. During his 1930 gubernatorial campaign, Chase urged others to look into the connection between Floyd B. Olson and Yiddish gangsters, with Chase's obsession moving from the theme of "Jew-gangsters" to that of "Jew-Communists."

After the 1936 landslide victory of the Democrats and the Farmer-Laborites, the Ray P. Chase Research Bureau was launched with offices in the Twin Cities, Chicago, and Washington, D.C. Funds were contributed to this effort by a list of individuals who represented the elite of Minnesota business. George L. Gillette, president of Minneapolis-Moline Company, acted as fund-raiser and received contributions from Jay C. Hormel, James Ford Bell, George K. Belden, Colonel Robert McCormick, and officers of the leading bank holding corporations in Minnesota. Among the stated purposes of the bureau were, and I'm quoting here, "to block the efforts of the present Governor and his communistic Jewish advisors to perpetuate themselves in power [and] to block efforts to initiate and promote in Minnesota the Soviet plan of Social Ownership of Key Industries."

There were two Republican campaigns in 1938, the high road and the low road. Harold Stassen spoke about issues, tried to out–New Deal the New Deal, and damned the special interests in language reminiscent of Floyd B. Olson; his followers described him as "truly Olson's heir." Stassen claimed that he would continue the Farmer-Labor social programs but run them more efficiently and fairly. He further promised to institute a program of civil service reform, labor reform, and social insurance that would combine the best of the New Deal with the best elements of business efficiency.

While Stassen took the high road, Chase and his friends plumbed the sewers. A whispering campaign was begun that sought to explain Jewish control over Benson by tracing it to his marriage bed. It was falsely rumored that Frances Miller Benson was Jewish. Benson's Communist support was emphasized as was his erratic behavior on the stump. The major campaign contribution of the Chase group, however, was a slick anti-Semitic pamphlet distributed en masse in early October titled "Are They Communists or Catspaws?"

This sixty-page pamphlet stressed the Jewishness of Benson's major aides. Their alleged Communist activities were outlined, most of the information coming from fascist groups and most of it blatantly false. The booklet, subtitled, "A Red Baiting Article by Ray P. Chase," concluded with an attack on Benson's appointments to the University of Minnesota Board of Regents and the regents' willingness to allow such Communists as the black poet Langston Hughes to declaim his anti-Christian poetry at the University.

Before the impact of this pamphlet could be fully gauged, a scurrilous cartoon was distributed throughout the state, blown up into posters and finally placed on giant billboards. This cartoon, titled "Three Jehu Drivers," shows a donkey with Governor Benson's face, being ridden by three Semitic-featured riders, Rutchick, Harris, and Jacobs, in the direction of rule or ruin. Around them are the forgotten men—the Yankees, Irish, Italians, Scandinavians, Germans, French, Polish, and others—holding up their hands and in one version asking, "When Do We Get On, Governor?"

Protests came into Stassen headquarters condemning the anti-Semitic nature of the campaign. Leading Minnesotans begged that he repudiate Chase's actions. Stassen remained silent. During the week prior to the election, a delegation of leading Jewish Republicans met with Stassen to ask him to do something. His response was to place an advertisement in the local Anglo-Jewish weekly, the *American Jewish World,* the day before the election but not once mentioning the reason for this kind of election eve piety.

Election day was anticlimactic. Stassen overwhelmingly defeated Benson, and Republicans captured every major state office. All Farmer-Labor congressmen but one were defeated in reelection bids, and the state legislature went overwhelmingly Republican. So ended the 1938 election and the most successful and disgusting use of political anti-Semitism in the United States.

It was on these dark moments in Minnesota history that Hubert Humphrey would build the human rights platform that would catapult him to national leadership and fame.

Remember, Carey McWilliams's article was published soon after evidence of the death camps in Germany and Poland began to sink in around the nation and in Minnesota. A year earlier, in 1945, Humphrey, that young former University of Minnesota student and former Macalester College political science instructor, was elected mayor of Minneapolis. Hubert saw McWilliams's piece, saw the newsreels of concentration camps in the movie theaters, and was appalled that his city was considered the capital of anti-Semitism. He was determined to wipe that out. A good number of his friends and colleagues in graduate school were Jews, including his best friend, Art Naftalin, who, of course, went on to become Minneapolis's first Jewish mayor in 1961 and was, before then, Hubert's chief administrative assistant.

Good politician that he was, the first thing Humphrey did in response to the McWilliams article was to appoint a blue ribbon committee to look into the facts, and he sort of skewed the commission by putting Naftalin in as chair. It was discovered that not only were there no Jewish teachers, there also were no Jewish policemen, no Jewish firemen, and hardly any Jewish clerks in city government. The committee made a report that created action. It seems simple now, but it wasn't then.

Hubert Humphrey, by executive order, helped create the Fair Employment Practices Commission, which led to the city council's passing an antidiscrimination bill that would prohibit the city government's denial of employment for anyone from different racial, ethnic, or religious backgrounds. This was the first giant step in Hubert's commitment to civil and human rights as the fundamental principle of his own philosophy.

In 1947, when the Americans for Democratic Action was formed by, among others, Eleanor Roosevelt, the United Auto Workers leader Walter

Reuther, and Hubert, the fundamental basis for the ADA was, in fact, to move to eliminate segregation and race prejudice from the legal, economic, social, and political system. The best way was to have a human rights plank in the Democratic Party platform of 1948 that would, in fact, lead to the beginning of the end of a segregated society.

And who led that fight? Humphrey, and it stemmed from his understanding of the depths of anti-Semitism in Minneapolis. It led to his central role at the 1948 Democratic National Convention, when the segregationist Southerners, opposed to an antisegregation plank in the Democratic platform, walked out of the convention and formed the Dixiecrat Party, led by the racist senator from South Carolina, Strom Thurmond. And, of course, Humphrey delivered his historic speech at the convention, the one I listened to back at City College when they were trying to fix my New York accent, an effort, as anyone who knows me can tell you, that failed miserably.

Hubert said, and these were brilliant words, words that would define the Democratic Party for the next sixty years and that lifted him to true national prominence, "My friends, to those who say that we are rushing this issue of civil rights, I say to them we are 172 years late. To those who say that this civil rights program is an infringement on states' rights, I say this: The time has arrived in America for the Democratic Party to get out of the shadow of states' rights and to walk forthrightly into the bright sunshine of human rights."

Ironically, in 1948 another Minnesotan actually ran for president in the Republican Party. That was Harold Stassen, he of the ugly 1938 gubernatorial election. Stassen, of course, lost, but Humphrey won big as he ran for the U.S. Senate and trounced the incumbent, Joseph Ball. Hubert won nearly 60 percent of the vote. Hubert was thirty-seven years old. He had so much in front of him.

Which takes us to 1964, and the Democratic Convention in Atlantic City. This was the convention in which Lyndon Johnson was finally going to be crowned president. After all, up until now, he was president because John F. Kennedy was killed. This was to be LBJ's convention. He was going to control it all, and Hubert Humphrey was one of the leading contenders for the nomination for vice president. Johnson had made that very clear, but there was a big hurdle before that could take place. And Hubert was supposed to help Johnson clear that hurdle.

The summer of 1964 was known as "Mississippi Freedom Summer," and the registration of black voters in Mississippi wasn't going too well, but well enough that they were able to mount a challenge to the established Democratic Party and its delegation to the Democratic National Convention. The belief was that the Mississippi delegation to the convention should be integrated. Fannie Lou Hamer was one of the most important figures in that challenge. She became so significant that her presence was frightening Lyndon Johnson. He didn't want her and her Freedom Party group to be credentialed and on the convention floor because she was so dynamic, dramatic, and compelling. Johnson wanted her out. He wanted a unified convention, and he didn't want to lose votes in other Southern states.

Johnson made it clear to Hubert, who was, after all, the civil rights advocate, that if Hamer's challenge weren't stopped—and if Hubert himself didn't stop that challenge—someone else, not Hubert, would be the vice presidential candidate. Hubert then went to Walter Mondale, who was the Minnesota attorney general, and asked Fritz to lead the battle so that the challenge could be somehow stopped.

A compromise was attempted. Essentially, we have the Mississippi Freedom Democratic Party delegation, an integrated delegation, and we had the official Mississippi delegation, which was not only white but also white supremacist. The compromise presented was that two of the Mississippi Freedom delegates would be put on the convention floor. But the official white delegation would remain. The others would be guests of the convention.

Obviously, this was not acceptable to the integrated delegation of Mississippi, so pressure was put on them by Humphrey, by union leader Walter Reuther, by Bayard Rustin, who organized the March on Washington a year earlier, and by A. Philip Randolph, the African American labor leader. In other words, it wasn't only the white establishment that was putting pressure on Fannie Lou Hamer. In the end, no compromise was agreed to and the Freedom delegates left Atlantic City empty handed.

The outcome was that LBJ was very happy and soon after, while Humphrey was still in Atlantic City, Johnson named him to be his running mate.

One of the changes that did take place as a result of all of these battles was that, from then on, there wouldn't be any more white supremacist delegations in the Democratic conventions. There would be integrated delegations only. In a sense, the Democrats began to move in the direction of identity politics for the first time and continue in that way to this day, for good or for ill. Humphrey was a force around that. And the pendulum of history swung. The anti-Semitism of Minnesota and, especially Minneapolis, that energized Humphrey led to the passage of the Civil Rights Act of 1964 and the Voting Rights Act of 1965, with Humphrey as a champion.

Which brings us back to 1968, and Hubert and the war and my initial opposition to him as a presidential candidate. The Vietnam War that I opposed was bubbling up. Lyndon Johnson was trying to get elected to a second term. The counterculture was in ascension, and it was all about to come together at the 1968 Democratic National Convention that summer. Amid this an unlikely hero emerged. Of all people, Gene McCarthy, the other Minnesota senator, got in Hubert's way to become president. McCarthy is the only one who, in 1967, challenged Johnson for the presidency, and LBJ was the president of McCarthy's own party. McCarthy was doing that because he opposed the war. This generated the kind of groundswell of support from people who had never even heard of Eugene McCarthy before. It was, you know, a "Children's Crusade," or that's what it was called because of all the young people who supported him.

So, McCarthy went to New Hampshire and campaigned widely in the primary and made a great showing, didn't beat Johnson, but came close. He scared the pants off Johnson and raised the kind of political ruckus in the Democratic Party that had never been seen before. He didn't scare him because Johnson thought he'd lose the next primary in Wisconsin, but because the Vietnam War as an issue was coming to a head and LBJ didn't want to face it as a candidate. Barely three weeks later, Johnson shocked the world and said he wouldn't run for president in 1968.

The landscape instantly and radically changed. Robert Kennedy, who refused to challenge the incumbent president of his own party, which is, of course, the conventional wisdom as far as political sense is concerned, now emerged. Kennedy captured the imagination of those who had been previously been left out of politics, marginal folks, minority folks. He did not, however, win that so-called Children's Crusade, those who had been with Gene McCarthy. So, Kennedy and McCarthy were fighting it out for the rest of the primary season.

Until, of course, Bobby Kennedy won the California primary and was assassinated that night. Civil rights leader Martin Luther King Jr. had been assassinated two months earlier. This was a nation coming apart. Then we went to Chicago for the Democratic National Convention where our Minnesota friend Hubert Humphrey was now the heir apparent for the established power base of the Democratic Party. He was no rebel. This man who fought against anti-Semitism and segregation, he was now the Establishment. It was the old guard versus new guard in Chicago, and, ironically, Hubert Humphrey became the symbol of the old guard. Boy, did that rankle him.

The streets, filled with demonstrators and rioters, turned into a catastrophe. The convention, televised nationally, turned into a zoo. The Democratic Party, trying to remain in power, looked out of control to a country divided. And Hubert, I'm afraid, didn't quite understand all that was going on around him. He had reached the peak of what he had wanted all his lifetime and he filtered everything out. Why else would he call his crusade "the politics of joy"? This wasn't a case of the politics of joy. This was the politics of disillusion in our nation at that time.

I know he told me later that he was appalled, but I really don't think at the time that it dawned on him, the depth of the controversy and the depth of the division that existed in the nation. He went out campaigning as the "Happy Warrior" and his campaign floundered.

But then something awful happened that energized his campaign. The racist governor of Alabama, George Wallace, ran for president on the American Independent Party ticket. The problem for Hubert posed by Wallace wasn't only that he was taking away Southern states. He was taking away blue-collar voters across the country. Humphrey now was faced with the dilemma of trying to recapture that Democratic base, and he did the best he could with the support of Reuther and the AFL-CIO.

Meanwhile, the Eugene McCarthy–Humphrey division persisted to Humphrey's dying days. McCarthy never fully endorsed Humphrey, which hurt Hubert. Remember, these were close friends and political allies before. So the 1968 presidential campaign came down to this. The

Republican nominee, Richard Nixon, claimed, "I've got a secret plan to end the war in Vietnam." So, he won both the war hawks and the war doves on that one. Then, Nixon had a Southern strategy to pick off Wallace votes. And his vice presidential candidate, Spiro Agnew, gave law-and-order speeches, which were symbols of racism, essentially. Add to that, Humphrey was faced with Lyndon Johnson and the escalating war on his back.

Finally, in late September, just weeks before Election Day, Humphrey broke with Lyndon Johnson over the war. He proposed in a Salt Lake City speech that, when he was elected, he'd stop the bombing in North Vietnam and enter into real negotiations to end the war. This, of course, changed the whole tone of the rest of the election campaign. But not enough, and Nixon, the son of a bitch, won.

What Humphrey told me, and I think many political observers agree, was that had there been one more week to the campaign, or if he had broken from LBJ one week earlier, we would be talking here about President Humphrey and not the Hubert Humphrey who almost was president.

As the spring and summer of 1968 unfolded, it became apparent to me that Humphrey might not win the election, and I started speaking to May Brodbeck, the Philosophy chair at the University of Minnesota, and to Frank Sorauf, the Political Science chair, who were members of the Advisory Committee of the Social Sciences program. "Wouldn't it be a good idea," I asked them, "if Hubert loses, to invite him to join, somehow or other, the faculty and either develop his own course or be a resource person for people in political science and history? At least both give him a chance to politically decompress and give us the opportunity to benefit from his experience?"

Frank was very, very unhappy with that kind of suggestion, and I'd find out why later. May was fairly happy. Paul Murphy, a legal history scholar, was on the Advisory Committee then, too, and he thought it was a good idea. Frank changed his mind very quickly after Humphrey's defeat, joined with the majority, and made it unanimous that we invite Hubert to the Social Sciences program. But not Frank's Political Science Department. Subsequently, I had to tell Hubert the reason for that, and he wasn't pleased.

As it turned out, the Political Science Department had voted almost unanimously not to accept Humphrey as a member of the faculty. They said that although he once had been a graduate student at the University, he never finished his dissertation, so didn't get his doctorate, and, lacking that credential, was unqualified to teach politics. I'm not kidding you. The guy had been a mayor, a U.S. senator, the architect of mainstream civil rights activism, and almost became president of the United States. If he'd won the White House, he still wouldn't have had his Ph.D. And he wasn't qualified to teach political science?

When Walter Heller, who was the head of President Kennedy's Council of Economic Advisers and now our top economics professor, heard about this, he couldn't believe it. He came running into my office and said, "Hy, is this true?"

"Walter, calm down."

He said, "That's an outrage. I'm going to raise holy hell." Heller protested to the president of the University and to the Regents, but, of course, departments have autonomy and all that. You can't break it.

Unbeknownst to me and other faculty members, there were other negotiations going on after the election. Later I learned from Hubert himself and from others that there had been conversations between President Moos and Humphrey and between University Regent Lester Malkerson and Humphrey. They were conversations on the upper level without any faculty input, which was a violation of our procedures right and left.

Soon, I got a call from Moos saying that Humphrey was going to be with me in the Social Sciences program. That was fine with me, of course. Humphrey agreed to join the faculty, and for the rest of his life he called me "Boss."

When Hubert Humphrey came onto the faculty, I lost even more friends than I lost when I announced I was supporting him for the presidency of the United States. They were temporary losses. Some, like my colleague and good friend Allan Spear, accused me of giving a platform to a war criminal, but it didn't prevent Spear from being the first to request the services of Hubert Humphrey in his classroom. A number of people resigned from our professors' Thirty-Niners Dining Club—a sort of drinking club for scholars—after I invited Hubert to come as my guest.

The first day Hubert came up to the Social Sciences Building, he came with the Secret Service, of course. Former vice presidents get that protection for a while after they're out of office. We arranged to have an office for him. It was a corner office and the Secret Service was upset with that. The exit route was very, very limited and our corridors very narrow. The Secret Service decided that the best way of handling an eventual emergency was to get a rope ladder to get out of the window. I ordered a rope ladder using the limited supply budget that we had. Then, we discovered that Hubert couldn't fit through that window.

All in all, I think the vice president's presence on campus was successful. He was well utilized in classes the first quarter or so. Then he developed his own courses. He taught a course in government and public policy on the undergraduate level. The enrollments had to be screened. They had some prerequisites. In the second year of his stay with us in the program, he became increasingly politically active. He began asserting his prerogatives as national leader of the Democratic Party. It was just at this time that he had ongoing commitments to meet the classes. It was fascinating to see how he was able to juggle those things and handle it. And he was teaching a course at Macalester College in St. Paul too.

Periodically, people would knock on my door, and I'd open it and there would be Senator Birch Bayh or Senator Henry "Scoop" Jackson or Hy Bookbinder, the powerful Washington lobbyist, unannounced and unheralded. They'd knock on my door and say, "I'm here to take Hubert's place today." He always made sure that someone covered his class when he was out.

The only really strained moment between Hubert and me came when he discovered that the Political Science Department had vetoed his appointment to the University when he first came on board, and that was why he was part of the Social Sciences program and not Political Science. He asked me, after he learned that, "Is it true?" He started getting angry with me. He said, "Why didn't you tell me?"

"Why should I tell you? What you don't know won't hurt you."

"But you should be honest with me. You should have told me."

"What difference would it have made?"

"I wouldn't have been so friendly with those SOBs. I feel like a fool."

"I wouldn't pay much attention to it," I said. "There are academic standards that they insist on and even though you are not going to teach graduate programs, they still feel that someone without a Ph.D. should not teach in their department. That's their prerogative. They have the right to do that. I think they're full of shit, but that's their prerogative. Don't get angry. Don't get upset. It's nothing against you. Any A.B.D. would be put in that position."

"What's an A.B.D.?"

"All But Dissertation. Isn't that your status?"

It was.

During the period of time we worked together and got to know each other, Hubert told me an interesting story about his relationship with Lyndon Johnson. They were not very close, and people who read the historical and political literature now know of Lyndon harassing Hubert and, really, dehumanizing him. But the worst story is one I haven't seen anywhere else. He told it to me in our house, and his wife, Muriel, was there and Betty was there. It shook me up a bit.

On inaugural night, the president and vice president of the United States traditionally go to different inaugural balls at different times of the evening and then they meet together at the main ball—I think it was the Washington Hilton—but they meet up very late in the evening. And when the ball was winding down, he said to Hubert, "Come over to the house for a nightcap." He called the White House "the house." Hubert and Muriel went over there to the residence, and they drank and they talked and they had an amiable conversation, and it was time to leave. Hubert headed toward the staircase leading down from the residence. As they were walking, the president had his arm around Hubert and he said to him, "Hubert, I want you to know that you have a constituency now of one, me. And I've got my hand in your pocket and my hand is on your balls, and one false fucking move out of you, I'll grab your balls out of their socket."

When he told that story, I was shocked. I knew about the vulgarity of Lyndon Johnson. It was well known, but I didn't know it went to that depth and to that level of cruelty, essentially. So I said to Hubert, "Weren't you shocked? What did you do? What did you feel?"

And he said, "Frankly, my hand was on his back and we were at the top of the stairs and running through my mind was, 'Should I throw the son of a bitch down the stairs?' But my mind went also to the next thought: 'What would happen if I did that?' The next day the headlines are, 'VICE PRESIDENT KILLS PRESIDENT, BECOMES PRESIDENT.' I don't think I could live with that."

A decade later, Hubert was dying of cancer, and a couple of days before he passed away I got a phone call from him at my house. I wanted to go out to Waverly to his place and visit with him. I just couldn't bring myself to do it, remembering him as the vigorous man he was. It was a touching moment. The phone rang and I picked it up. It was Hubert's weak voice.

He said, "Hi, Boss. I just wanted to check in with you. How are things going?"

5
Rupees and Burps
Going International

My first international travel came in 1964, just three years after arriving at Minnesota. It started a series of teaching and lecturing in India, China, and Germany that gave me new perspectives on communism and on life. I'd already subtly denounced the false gods of communism in my 1952 *Historia Judaica* book review, but traveling abroad made me appreciate the United States and Minnesota in a new light.

It all started with the University's contract with the State Department to help set up an American studies operation at Osmania University in Hyderabad, India. And, no, that city isn't named after me! The program was funded by Public Law 480. I mention this because this was a typical Hubert Humphrey contribution as a senator. Hubert drafted PL 480, which President Dwight Eisenhower renamed the "Food for Peace" bill. The idea was to sell U.S. grain to Third World nations using their own currency, which made it cheaper. And, then, the money used to buy the food would stay in India to enhance education. That's how I understood that it worked. It was nonmilitary foreign aid. Very Hubert-like, and we were the only university involved at that point.

When I got there, I was treated like royalty. I was paid in rupees, not dollars, in India, and I had more rupees than the maharaja of Hyderabad. I mean, I was rolling in rupees. I had servants who had servants. I never lived so well in my life. I had a friend who was an entrepreneur and he had a tailor who made his clothes, Indian-style clothes. He made some for me too. Imagine me in those long shirts like Gandhi.

Anyway, because I was more or less in the neighborhood, I decided to make my first trip to Israel after my teaching work in India. I walked off the plane in Tel Aviv dressed in an Indian suit and I must have looked like a mess, like I was coming from Mars. But I got through customs there and the first thing the customs official did was look at my dress. "Welcome to your country. You're at home now." That was the line in those days. I was Jewish. He could tell from my passport that I was Jewish, I guess, and he said, "You are home now." I looked in the mirror and said, "My God, I don't look Jewish. I look Indian." By the way, I quickly changed my clothes to my old clothes as soon as I got to a place to change.

I got to Israel and stayed with Betty's aunt and met many of Betty's relatives. This is the aunt that Betty spent the entire Shoah years with, first, in the Lodz ghetto, then in Auschwitz, in Stutthof, in Dresden, and then they escaped into Czechoslovakia when it was liberated. This aunt went off to Israel and Betty came to the United States. They went through hell together, but they separated. Getting to know her was great.

She treated me like royalty, too, but not in rupees. She cooked. My God, what food! After being starved in India, I was finally fed in Israel, of all places. She made the best cheese danishes I ever ate. I couldn't get my fill of them they were so great. So that was my stay in Israel.

You know, I had never considered myself a Zionist. I was always an internationalist, not a nationalist. I saw the solution with the Jewish problem as being the solution of a class problem, a typical Marxist analysis, and downplaying nationalism. I foresaw the problem with Zionism of trying to build up a nation in an alien environment, as being something that would be very difficult. I was never a Zionist. I'm still not.

And I resisted becoming what I'd call Minnesota's "professional Jew." That is, one who is institutionally involved in the Jewish community to the extent that he represents the Jewish community and is professionally identified also as a Jew, and, sometimes, only as a Jew. Although, in many ways and in many different forms, I was very much involved and actively involved in the Jewish community right from the start when I came to Minnesota, I don't think I have ever been identified that way by my peers here in Minnesota, and I never perceived myself as such.

There were certain times when the tensions between the Jewish community and me were rocky. I'm thinking particularly of the 1968–70 period. That was after I returned from Berkeley and all hell broke loose on Minneapolis's North Side, which still had a large Jewish presence. I pointed out at every opportunity that this was in part a function of the tensions that built up between an incoming group of people who see themselves as deprived and an outgoing group, who have actually been deprived and have made it. I made this kind of analysis in a number of different venues. I pointed out that the objects of the ire of black uprising on Plymouth Avenue were the Jewish stores that remained, and they were perceived, really, as exploitative.

In saying that, I was not seen as too much of a friend of the Jewish community. Nor was I seen as a friend when I became actively involved with many other members of the Jewish community in questioning some of the policies of the Israeli government. I also was frequently asked to talk about the Middle East and I did, in terms of the tragic conflict between peoples with equal rights to the same land, and obviously, this caused some of the Jewish community to tear their hair out, insofar as they had any hair left.

Still, when the Minnesota Historical Society Press put together its series on Minnesota ethnic communities, I was asked to do the one on the Jews in Minnesota. That identified me as being *the* Jew in Minnesota, I guess, but I wasn't.

Looking back, my political work in New York and my academic work were connected with Jewish issues. My connections to my mentor, Salo Baron, the leading historian of the Jewish people, highlighted that. The interconnections between the Jewish immigrant community and the Communist Party–related schools, camps, and organizations confirmed that. My upbringing speaking Yiddish was undeniable.

That's why I had one really very interesting decision to make early in my career. In the midsixties, I got a letter from the president of the American Jewish Historical Society. They were looking for and wanted a professional director of the society, and the board of directors had all decided that I was the one they wanted. This was without having an interview or anything like that. Of course, they knew me and I knew them. I wrote a letter back saying this was intriguing so let's follow this through. I got a subsequent letter outlining conditions and salary, which was double what I was making here at the University. Of course, I would have had to live in New York, which was more expensive than here, but it came with tremendous responsibilities and, even, visibility.

I was debating with myself whether to do that. But I knew that if I took the position then I would be a professional Jew.

Salo Baron got on the phone with me. In one call he urged me to take it. The second phone call he urged me not to take it. He was following through the same kind of reasoning that I was going through. Finally, I decided not to take it. I could have left Minnesota, lived in New York, been a professional Jew, been in the Jewish establishment, probably would have done very, very well as director of the American Jewish Historical Society. Eventually, the society opened a branch in Boston; I could have developed a professorship up there. It would have been all nice, but life would have been completely different. I would not have been able to do what I did with Rudy in the governor's office, I would not have known Hubert Humphrey, I would not have had the kind of international experiences that I did at Minnesota. So it would have been quite different, but I had that opportunity then and I decided to stay.

I'm glad I did, and I've seen changes in the way Jews are accepted in the Twin Cities community. We have come a long way since I arrived and, certainly, since the Carey McWilliams article of 1946. It took struggle and political stick-to-itiveness, but there is full acceptance—I'm not saying it's perfect—of the Jewish community within the city of Minneapolis, and I'm happy about that.

I do know, though, that when Betty and I moved here in 1961 and we were looking for a house, we asked about Wayzata. I don't know why, but we did. And the real estate agent said, "Oh, no, your people don't move there." And I said, "We don't move there because we're not allowed to move there."

Sibley and China

I had a successful semester in India, and when I came back to the Minnesota campus the question was who was going to succeed me in the Osmania program the next year. We had a meeting with the faculty of the American Studies program and it was decided that Mulford Sibley would go. Mulford was well known at that time for his socialist, pacifist, and free love views. He was very outspoken and already had been fired at Stanford for his views. We thought he'd be a great person to go and the Political Science Department was happy to see him go. They didn't particularly care for him. He was doing what's called normative political science, always analyzing values and how the world should look and be. The others were doing mathematical political science, always looking at data and analyzing what was happening on the ground.

So, everything was all set and getting close to his leaving, but Mulford didn't have his visa yet. Charles Frankel, a philosopher whom I knew at Columbia, had become the under secretary of state for education. I gave him a call and he said to me, "My God, didn't anybody inform you people in Minnesota?"

"What?"

"Well, Mulford Sibley was blacklisted. The Board of Foreign Scholarships headed by Oscar Handlin of Harvard had said that Mulford Sibley is too subversive to be an American representative in India."

"That's ridiculous. I'm going to try and do something about it."

So I called Norman Sherman, who was Hubert Humphrey's press secretary. And Hubert was the vice president of the United States by then. Norman had been a student of Mulford's at one point. Norman said, "I agree it's ridiculous. I'm going to tell Hubert. Mulford is a good friend of Hubert's." Soon after, Hubert got on the phone and told me, "I'll take care of it."

A week passed, two weeks passed, three weeks passed, nothing happened. Finally, there was a phone call from Norman, who said, "Hubert can't do a thing."

"What?"

"Hold on a moment, Hubert wants to talk to you."

He got on the phone and I said, "Yes, Mister Vice President."

Hubert responded, "I pulled all the strings I could. I even got to President Johnson and said, 'Let's pull some strings.' But Oscar Handlin is adamant and the Board of Foreign Scholarships is an autonomous body, and we can't do anything about it."

Handlin wasn't a right-winger, no. He was what I would call a Cold War liberal. There's a difference. Mulford rubbed those Cold War liberals the wrong way because Mulford believed in freedom without any kind of restraint, you know. And he was vehemently opposed to any involvement in Vietnam. We decided not to send anyone the next year.

It took me awhile for my next international adventure. My first trip to China was in the summer and early fall of 1981. It came soon after the University's first higher education delegation went to China in 1979. It was headed by the chair of the Board of Regents, Wenda Moore, who, fortunately, was black. Perfect—a black chair of the Board of Regents of the University of Minnesota. Imagine that! One of the people in the delegation was Ted Farmer from my History Department, a modern Chinese historian.

When they got to China, they asked what we at the U could do for them. Of course, they needed a lot of technical stuff, scientific stuff, agricultural stuff, but then, all of a sudden, they said they also wanted to get reacquainted with American history, preferably through teaching labor history. So, Ted Farmer said, "We've got a labor historian at the University of Minnesota." "Who is that?" they asked. It was me. Upon their return, neither Ted nor Regent Moore told me about this exchange.

Three or four months after they came back, I got a registered letter from Beijing, asking me to come to China to reopen access to U.S. history by teaching a continuing series of lectures for five months at Nankai University. Leading Chinese scholars in American history from across China would come together for my lectures. A few of the older ones had trained at Stanford, Berkeley, and Columbia. That was before World War II. The ones who were trained as American historians in the 1950s attended universities in Moscow and St. Petersburg. So, they had a Soviet interpretation of American history.

Then, for twenty years, they had no interpretation of American history at all because it was forbidden in China during the Cultural Revolution. Their books in the U.S. history section of the university libraries ended in around 1960. I'm not exaggerating. I came there in '81. That's a twenty-year gap of interpretation and understanding.

Ronald Reagan had just become U.S. president and the State Department Reaganites were actually pretty smart. They gave me a budget to buy American history books to build up the library at Nankai University. I exceeded the budget they gave me more than three or four times. I said, "What should I do?" They told me to continue exceeding the budget. I built up a library. The Reagan people were smart.

The University of Minnesota has had a long role in Chinese higher education. The first Chinese students came to the U in Minneapolis in 1914. Many of the leaders who emerged after the Cultural Revolution in higher education circles in China were once students at the U. The higher education authorities in China were looking to work out some kind of academic contacts within the United States.

I got to China, and it was a very primitive time. The professor who greeted me was named Yang Shengmao. He had received his doctorate at, I think, Stanford University in the early 1940s and taught for a while at Berkeley. In '45 he went back to China to help in the revolution because he was a member of the Chinese Communist Party. But he eventually became one of the first victims of the Cultural Revolution. He was sent to the countryside, had a kind of dunce hat put on, and was paraded in front of his students, but he survived.

Eventually, they put him in charge of what they called the American History Research Section. Yang and I worked together for about five months at Nankai. I met some of the top people when they came there, and of course they went back to their own institutions afterward. So that was my first and longest stay in China.

To be sure, Mao period hangovers were still there because at the end of my stay they thanked me profusely for my bourgeois interpretation of history. To make sure that all these great scholars would get the right interpretation, they invited Philip Foner to come and clean up my act. Phil, of course, was at City College before I got there, was blacklisted for alleged connections to the U.S. Communist Party, and was considered far more left wing than I. But since they didn't know what Phil looked like, they asked me to go to Beijing airport with them to pick up Phil, whom I knew very well.

This was still early China. It was before any kind of great security stuff, so we went onto the tarmac. We had a red carpet that we put down in front of the plane, and we made sure that Phil and his wife, Roslyn, would be the first ones off the plane. How they arranged that I don't know, but they did.

Phil and Roslyn came down the tarmac onto the red carpet, and who's standing in front of the Chinese delegation but me. "Professor Philip Foner," I said, "I welcome you here to China in the name of the people of China." Phil looked at me. "What the fuck are you doing here, Hy?" I said, "Don't you know? You're here to clean up my act. You're to make sure that my political revisionism is put straight." He laughed. The Chinese thought of me as some kind of progressive despite their having described me as a bourgeois historian.

Let me divide this into segments. The academic side, which is what I did in 1981, was strictly that. But in 1981, I did meet some people from the All-China Federation of Trade Unions, which is now the largest union in the world with something like 100 million members, and, of course, leaders of the Communist Party. It was immediately thereafter that I got an invitation to go back to China from a group called the Chinese Association for International Understanding, and to deliver lectures on American history.

I knew the lectures were important as soon as I walked into the room. In previous talks there, I would lecture, sit down, and someone would get up and translate. It took forever. In this case, unlike that one, there was a booth in the back. Each seat had earphones and there were two interpreters sitting in the back simultaneously translating into microphones. I knew this was important stuff. Then, when the audience moved in, I knew even more that it was important stuff. I recognized some of the people. I'd seen them on television, greeting productive workers and model communes. Those were big shots who had come to these lectures.

I gave the lectures on the history of American communism, and they made a big hit. But during the question-and-answer session afterward, someone said I should cut the bullshit. This was all in Chinese, so I don't think they used the word "bullshit." The interpreter didn't use the word "bullshit," but I was able to infer that that was what they were saying. They would demand: "Give us the essence. What was the relationship, what is the relationship, between the American Communist Party and the Soviet Party. Put it in plain language."

I said to myself, OK, if these guys want the truth I'll give them the truth about the U.S. C.P.'s leader Gus Hall, who was from Minnesota, and Soviet President Leonid Brezhnev, who had just died. So I said, "The only way I can define the relationship between the U.S. party and the Soviet Union is this: When Brezhnev has indigestion, Gus Hall burps."

The place roared. There were two levels of laughter, first the ones who understood English, and then after the translation. It was remarkable. It opened up from then on. Of course, the burp is important culturally and even acceptable in China, so that added quite a bit to it. I think that was my favorite and most critical contribution to the Chinese understanding of American communism.

I returned to Nankai University in 1987 and I assumed I'd go in 1989. But I wasn't invited, and I didn't go after that for many years. In 1995 the University of Minnesota was invited to send a delegate to the ninetieth anniversary of Fudan University in Shanghai and I was selected. When it became known that I was going to China, I got a telephone call from Beijing, from one of the people who was kind of a middle-level party official whom I had gotten to know after he came to Minnesota.

"I see you're going to be in China representing the University," he said. "I want you to reserve three or four days to spend with us in Beijing."

"I'm sorry, but I already made my plane reservations and, you know, Northwest Airlines is not going to change anything."

"Leave that to us," he replied.

Two days later, I got a call from Northwest saying, "We changed your reservations and upgraded you to business class." So, I got back there and I did spend the last three days in Beijing as a guest of now top people in the Communist Party. They showed me a great time and I gave one lecture at the Chinese Academy of Social Sciences. At the end of my stay, my last night, they asked if I was all packed and ready to go. And I was. I was told someone would pick up my bags and take me to the airport in the morning, which they did. They took me right to the plane.

A guy who looked like he was from the Secret Service or FBI took me on the plane before anyone else was on there. He said, "Let's talk frankly. Do you know why you weren't invited back to China for the past seven years?"

"No."

"Well, you know the Tiananmen Square uprising in 1989? Some of the leaders of that group were in your graduate seminar at Nankai University in 1987. And we assumed that you contaminated them."

"Hold on a moment. You had your spies in my classroom? Obviously, you wouldn't let me teach advanced students without having spies there. But didn't they tell you that when we talked about political science my words to them were words of caution, that change does not take place overnight? It's slow and steady? Your informants, your spies, are either liars, fools, or don't understand English."

Of course, in a U.S. history course we talked about American civil liberties and even civil disobedience. There were about twenty-five students, and we talked about how open American politics are and how they translate to China.

The discussion had gone on with this agent of some sort for a while when he said, "We believe you, Professor Berman. Our informants were either liars, fools, or dupes. And we feel obliged to invite you to put together a high-level delegation of Minnesota political figures and bring them to China sometime soon."

But I never went back.

On to Europe

My European experiences began in 1984 when the University of Minnesota and the Ludwig Maximilian University in Munich worked out a faculty exchange program. The focal point of the exchange was the America Institute in Munich, and therefore it's not surprising that they would be primarily interested in Americanists here in the United States. I gave a number of seminars that focused mainly on American labor and social history.

Fortunately, I was able to find a wonderful apartment right in the heart of Schwabing, which is the Greenwich Village of Munich, the heart of the academic and cultural nightclub mix. Also, it was across the park from the Mensa, which is the dining hall of the university. The faculty dining hall was just magnificent. They had wonderful meals for very little money.

I was immediately brought into the academic atmosphere and made a member of the faculty. I was asked to participate on doctoral exam committees and I was even brought in as a member of the academic council with full voting rights. We don't do that for our visiting professors here at the University of Minnesota. I gave two seminars that I taught in English. I was so successful in 1984 that the German Fulbright Commission asked me to come back as a Fulbright professor at Ludwig Maximilian in 1985, which I agreed to do.

Ronald Reagan was the U.S. president in 1985. Most people know him as being an actor and not a very good one. While I was there, Reagan accepted an invitation from Chancellor Helmut Kohl to visit a German military cemetery near Bitburg. The problem was that a bunch of SS members were buried there, and Reagan had no intention of visiting any concentration camps where millions of Jews and others had been slaughtered. This caused, as you can imagine, a furor around the world and not just in the United States.

In Germany a number of my German colleagues got together on the day Reagan was going to Bitburg and they decided that we would go to Dachau, the notorious death camp just outside Munich. Not that we thought we were going to do anything there, but we'd feel good about ourselves. We would go to Dachau when this son of a bitch, our president, was going to be with the SS and their son of a bitch chancellor. Yes, their son of a bitch was going to be with my son of a bitch and they would both be kowtowing to the Nazi sons of bitches that are buried at Bitburg. So we went to Dachau as a symbolic gesture.

We got there and discovered that we weren't the only ones who thought the way we did. I remember a whole group came from England, including a Jewish member of Parliament, and they actually conducted a sort of memorial ceremony there. And, of course, there was a television crew there from New York City. Anything Jewish would go over big in New York. The television guy, as he walked in, recognized I was an American.

"Are you an American?" he asked.

"Yes."

"Can I interview you?"

"Sure."

"Where are you from?"

"Minnesota."

"Forget about it," he said. He wanted a New Yorker. Like me when I was a New Yorker, he never heard of Minnesota.

On the way back to Munich, when we got to the place where everybody dispersed to different subways to go home, for some reason I wanted to get a wurst, so I stopped at a wurst stand. There was a drunken German there who started screaming at me in German. "What's all this fuss they're making about Bitburg and Dachau? More Germans were killed than Jews." I said to him in good German, "Yeah, that's true, but remember that the Jews were killed by the Germans for being Jews. The Germans were killed in the army because they were trying to kill Jews, Americans, and British." He thought for a while and said, "Yeah, I guess that's true." That was my shot for good thought among drunks.

He probably forgot the next day that he had the conversation, but I felt good about it.

In the same vein, I had spoken with many colleagues at Munich about my work with Salo Baron and Jewish history, so they were very much interested, and when I became a Fulbright professor they wanted me to give a seminar on the Jewish labor movement, which would deal essentially with *Yiddishkeit* in America. That is, Jewish culture in America and, mostly Jewish first- and second-generation Americans like me, which I did.

It was very popular. My first group of students numbered in the sixties or seventies. There was a feeling, shall we say, that this was the generation after the generation that was responsible for the Holocaust. It was their parents who were involved and they were trying to atone for their parents, I think, so anything Jewish very much interested them.

I was also pretty good at marketing. I gave a lecture to the university community that I called "The People, the Language, and the Culture That Were Destroyed by the German Beasts." I figured that was a good, provocative title, and it was. The rector of the university asked me to give the speech in the same large lecture room where Hitler presided over the process by which the University of Munich became *Judenrein,* or "clean of Jews," in 1933 or '34. So I gave my Fulbright lecture from the same dais that Hitler used in presiding over the de-Jewification of the university in Munich, except that my lecture was on the damn Germans who destroyed Yiddish and the whole Jewish culture and the Jewish people.

In fact, while I was there, there was a revival of Yiddish in Germany, of Jewish *klezmer* music, and Jewish folk music. It was part of a vibrant experience. The Yiddish folk theater from Warsaw came and performed in Munich at that time. I went to the performance and I was chagrined to learn that the only Jew in the acting collective that came was the director. The others were Poles who kind of mouthed Yiddish.

As I said, the first year I conducted my classes in English, and then the second year I gave them the option to respond in English or German. If it was more complex and they couldn't do it in English, they could do it in German. I could understand. When I started dreaming in German, I thought that was the time to go home. I'd been in Germany too long. I was getting too comfortable there. And you could be comfortable there. Academics are treated very nicely in Germany.

Let me backtrack a bit. As you know, my wife, Betty, is a Holocaust survivor. So when I received the invitation to teach in Germany I was a bit reluctant. Soon after I got the invite, I happened to be on the phone with Salo Baron. We had other things we were talking about, but I told him, "You know, I'm not sure whether I want to go to Munich and I'm not sure I want to go to Germany at all." Baron had done his part to put the dagger in Nazism by being the chief historical witness in the war crimes trial of one of the biggest sons of bitches of all time, Adolf Eichmann, one of the architects of the Holocaust.

Baron said, "Oh, I've been to Germany many times. Look, I have no great love for them, but I go there in a feeling of triumphalism. Why don't you do that too?" That wasn't too difficult a convincing job that he had to do because I had already made up my mind I was going to go.

But I told him I had a big problem. "Betty. How do I get her to go back to Germany?" Baron said, "Put her on the phone." She got on the phone and a half hour later she got off and said, "I'm coming with you to Germany." I don't know what he told her. The first year I was in Germany, she was with me the whole time. She took leave from her work with the Minneapolis Public Library. The second time I went back, she refused to come. She just came and visited me once for a two- or three-week period. That first year, she was in part uncomfortable but increasingly became more comfortable. She resented the affluence of Germany and Munich, feeling that they should be more contrite and less affluent, but she enjoyed the affluence too. She enjoyed the good restaurants, she enjoyed the good music, she enjoyed the wonderful apartment we had. But she had had enough of Germany. I understood.

But I went back. The Munich experience was a good one for the University of Minnesota and for the university in Munich. Because of that, the University of Minnesota thought it should expand its German contacts and, through some people in our German Department, we had relationships with Humboldt University in what was then East Berlin. Humboldt University wanted to get some kind of Western contacts, to be out of East German isolation or at least European isolation. Of course, they had a great deal of contact with Moscow, Leningrad, and Warsaw, places like that, but not with Minnesota or the West.

We weren't yet ready to open up full arrangements with them, so the University of Minnesota proposed that since I had been in Munich, a month as a visiting professor at Humboldt University was worth a try. I was put in the section of Humboldt's History Department dealing with the history of the international working-class movements. Remember, this was a Communist society. International working-class movements for them meant Communist and socialist history. Obviously, the faculty in that department were dedicated Communists, and that's where they put me.

But there was an objection to my going. A number of people knew I was one of the founders of the Historians of American Communism and that I had gone to China. And then there was my University colleague, Erwin Marquit, the Physics Department Communist, who spent his summers at Humboldt University. It was his home away from home and his academic place of comfort. Let me just say, we weren't pals. When he heard I was going to be a visitor at Humboldt, he protested vehemently.

Fortunately, my friend Phil Foner, who seems to have followed me wherever I went, was teaching at Humboldt too. Phil told me that when the invitation was about to be issued to me, he happened to be in the Humboldt rector's office. The rector is like the university president. The rector wanted a Good Housekeeping Seal of Approval for me from Phil, and Phil gave it. But Marquit was there, too, and, Phil told me, Erwin ran into the rector's office and said, "Don't invite Hy Berman, he's a fascist." To which Foner responded, and again, this is Phil telling the story, "If Hy is a fascist, then there's no hope for progressive politics in the United States." At which point, the rector turned to Erwin and said, "We're inviting him," and I got there.

The ideological focus of Humboldt's History Department could be seen in the fact that a dissertation was done on the Socialist Workers Party in the United States and its impact on the peace movement, or the antiwar movement. The student writing the dissertation very meticulously went through the sources that he was allowed to go through and came to the conclusion that Trotskyists were a leading force in the antiwar movement in the United States. Pretty funny.

At his doctoral defense I raised the question as to what his sources were and whether he was able to go through any of the materials of Students for a Democratic Society or the Student Nonviolent Coordinating Committee, or any of the others. He said that he wasn't. I turned to my colleagues and I said, "This is a political contradiction." I knew how to use Marxist terminology and when to sling it around, if necessary. "This is a political contradiction," I continued. "You prevented him from seeing sources that would have allowed him to come to a conclusion that would be different from your ideological position. The Trotskyists were not at the center of the antiwar movement. It just seemed that way from the sources that your student read."

That caused a big furor in the defense of the dissertation. I hoped the upset it caused would lead to a more open access to sources for graduate students. Whether it did or not, I don't know because I left before I was able to see that. I pointed out a very important ideological shortcoming of their way of life. I felt good about it. I felt very good about it. One for the cause.

There was one Friday or Saturday when they had a party at which I was the guest of honor and somehow Erich Honecker, the leader of East Germany's Socialist Unity Party and the country's strongman, was there, and I was introduced to him. I had the chance to talk with him. I found it very fascinating that, yes, these guys are rigid and controlling, but they had a sense of humor.

At this party, with Honecker sitting there, they told a story that went something like this, if I can remember it accurately. Erich Honecker was driving back from Berlin to this place where we were, outside Berlin, and his driver accidentally hit a youngster on a bicycle. So they stopped the car, and Honecker ran to the kid to see what he could do to help him. He saw that the boy was not badly hurt but stunned, and the boy looked up and said, "Comrade Honecker, it's an honor for me to be hit by you."

As the story goes, Honecker felt relieved that the boy was OK and he said, "Where do you go to school?" The kid told him, and Honecker asked, "Are you a member of the Free German Youth?"

"Oh yes."

"When you become older, are you going to become a member of the Socialist Unity Party?"

"Oh, Comrade Honecker, I was hurt in my foot, not in my head."

Another story was told about Honecker going off to Moscow, and he came back and discovered that East Germany was gone. He was driving out of Berlin, and as he was leaving East Berlin, there was a sign, "Herr Honecker, when you leave the city, turn off the lights." Again, laughter.

Both times, these were told with Honecker sitting there, and he laughed like everyone else. They had a great sense of humor. Or maybe they knew the end was almost upon them. It was '87. Two years later they were gone.

I started thinking that if this was thirty-five years before, 1952 instead of 1987, and this was Moscow, the guys telling these jokes would be dead. Stalin wouldn't allow such a thing. At that point, I started feeling a little bit better. They had this sense of humor. At least they knew they were not in the strong position everybody else thought they were in. That's the only way I can interpret the fact that they were willing to accept, within their own circles to be sure, the jokes and the fact that they were told in my presence, me, an outsider.

Another interesting East Berlin story. There was a young man at Humboldt University who was a professor of political economy and who was a central person in the efforts to publish a new collected works of Karl Marx. He was working with the Soviet Academy of Sciences. It was a joint project. He was going back and forth between Moscow and East Berlin.

Over the course of our conversations, it became very clear that this young man was more than what he seemed to be. He gave me a couple of articles he'd written that were not for public consumption, which were highly critical of the East German economy. He had written a monograph that was very, very critical that he asked me to smuggle out when I left, to take it to a publisher in Munich, where I would be going, and I agreed to do it. It scared the shit out of me, but I did it.

He personally took me to the remnants of the Sachsenhausen concentration camp, a horrible place, and to the big Jewish cemetery in Berlin. I met his wife and his family, and it was clear to me he was about to defect.

The next day, I was about to leave. The woman who was in charge of the guesthouse where I was staying was a hard-line Communist Stalinist. She looked Stasi. She's the one who told me I should read the new issue of *Deutsche Einheit*, which was their political affairs theoretical journal. When I looked at the lead article I almost puked, because the lead article was written by "the most authoritative Marxist theoretician of the English language," Gus Hall. I knew Gus Hall very well. An authoritative theoretician he was not. In fact, he couldn't even spell the word.

Anyway, I thought I would have some fun. I was leaving. On the one hand, I was scared because I was taking out this manuscript. On the other hand, I was going to have some fun. I walked into the breakfast room with the daily newspaper. Every day we got the newspaper in front of our door. I walked up to Frau whatever-her-name was and said, "I think there's a mistake. I got yesterday's paper today."

"There's no mistake. You got today's paper." She grabbed it and said, "See the date—that's today's paper!"

"Oh yes, my mistake," I said. "Everything looks the same as yesterday's." She looked perturbed and then she blew up. She knew exactly what I was saying, and she called me a fascist. She called me a provocateur.

Soon after, I went to the Friedrichstrasse station to get back to West Berlin. I went into the station, went through customs and all that procedure, which was made easy by the fact that I had official documents. I still felt uneasy because in my bag was this manuscript. The first station we stopped at in West Berlin I got out. It was not the station where I had to get off. I just got off and went upstairs to breathe some air because I felt finally liberated and free. I was frightened, of course, at what I was doing. The audacity I had to do these things. If Betty were with me I never would have done these things. But two or three weeks after I left, I was told that the wife of the Humboldt University student who gave me the manuscript had been called in by the authorities. She taught at Humboldt University as well, and was told that if she didn't divorce her husband she would lose her job. Although he wasn't arrested, he was under surveillance. His party connections were broken. He was expelled from the party.

I was only there a month, but here's what I took away from that East German experience. When I was there, I was very much aware of being a former Communist. This was not new for me. I'd had that before. I'd had that in China before. This was my second international Communist experience, but my first experience with my kind of communism, not yellow communism. So, therefore, I felt both at home and, oddly but particularly, uncomfortable. This was like going back home in the Communist movement. I didn't like it.

6 "Rudy, You're Full of Shit"

I met Rudy Perpich and his family during some of my first months in Minnesota. A few years later, I was conducting research at the Minnesota Historical Society and began to have lunch regularly with three state senators who were still in their thirties and all pretty wet behind their ears: Wendell Anderson, Nick Coleman, and, yes, Rudy Perpich. I was still a junior member of the faculty, and I got to know these guys very well.

By 1970 the gubernatorial election cycle became of great interest to me because I knew all three who were running for governor and lieutenant governor on the DFL side. Anderson and Coleman were both running for the DFL endorsement and so was a colleague of mine from the University of Minnesota Law School, David Graven. And Perpich was running for the DFL's endorsement for lieutenant governor. Those were the days when there wasn't a unified ticket, but separate runs for each position.

In the end, Wendy and Rudy won the endorsement and the general election, so I had friends in high places. By 1974 the rules had changed; Anderson and Perpich ran on a unified governor–lieutenant governor ticket and were reelected. My friends remained in high places and I consulted with them on matters big and small, like when Rudy, as lieutenant governor, oversaw the state's U.S. Bicentennial festivities and I cautioned not to be so enthusiastic about painting every Port-a-John red, white, and blue. This was all good for me, but then things got complicated.

In 1976 Minnesotan Walter Mondale became vice president of the United States running on the ticket with Jimmy Carter. That left the U.S.

Senate seat Mondale held open. The decision had already been made but not gone public that Wendell Anderson was going to step down as Minnesota's governor, Lieutenant Governor Perpich would become governor, and, as part of the deal, Rudy would appoint Anderson as Mondale's replacement in Washington.

Oy!

After the inside decision was made, I got a phone call from Rudy. He asked me whether I'd be willing to assist him in any way he wished when he was governor. I said, "Of course. What do you want me to do?" He said, "The first thing I want you to do is get some corned beef and pastrami tomorrow over at your house and Lola and I will come over and have lunch with you and Betty." Because I'm a believer in ethnic reciprocity and had received a great deal of Croatian gastronomic enjoyment in the Perpich household in years past, I figured that we would reciprocate—or retaliate, as the case may be.

He and Lola came over, the dog barked at him, and I said, "You can't bark at the first Iron Range governor in Minnesota history." But he did and then we sat down and Rudy asked me to do two things for him in the transition period. One was to get together, insofar as possible, a congenial advisory group from the University faculty to assist him on economic and other policy matters; and the second thing he asked me to do was to be at his beck and call, part of the kitchen cabinet, historian in residence.

I said, "Fine," not knowing that it would result in two full-time jobs during the two years I was with him. In the course of that conversation, I also said, "I'd better check with the University administration and my department before I do anything like this." Everyone was fine with it as long as I taught my courses and fulfilled my committee obligations. I called University president Peter Magrath and, being the political animal he was, he simply wanted to know more about Perpich. I think he saw my role in the administration as an opportunity for the U.

It didn't always turn out that way because what was on Rudy's mind was also generally on his tongue. He never really thought through what he was about to say. I think of the initial meeting between him and Magrath, which began with Rudy saying his son was not going to the University. When Peter asked why not, Rudy replied, "Because it's too big, too impersonal, and too undistinguished. He's going to go to a smaller institution," to what was then the College of St. Thomas. Peter got very angry. He started shouting and finally stood up in a belligerent mood. I had to split up the men because Rudy was getting angry too. He would have punched Peter.

Of course, what Peter should have said was what I had been telling Rudy: "Yes, the University looks impersonal, large, and grand, but it's an institution with small units. And each unit is self-contained. If your son becomes a history major, he'll be with all these history people and be a part of a small community."

But that was Rudy and when he came over to the house for that pastrami he was very excited about the possibility of being governor. He never believed that he would ever be able to become governor. A Croatian Iron Ranger governor? His becoming governor was obviously a quirk, but he and I were both willing to accept the quirks of circumstance.

I must say that a few weeks before this, I would go to the Capitol cafeteria and very often would have lunch with the Anderson gubernatorial staff. During these lunchtime conversations, there was a discussion of whether, in fact, it would be politically prudent for Wendell to resign and become senator. During these discussions, I made it very clear to Tom Kelm, Anderson's chief of staff, and others that historically this never worked. Every governor who had ever resigned to become senator was forgotten after the next election because people didn't like that. Wendell Anderson was so popular that he could have sent Mickey Mouse in to fulfill the last two years of Mondale's term. Then Mickey Mouse would decide not to run, graciously withdrawing, and Wendell Anderson would run and win overwhelmingly and be the U.S. senator from Minnesota forever. But they didn't listen to me.

Fortunately, my advice didn't get back to Rudy because, if Rudy had learned what I said, he would have been very angry with me. He would have said very simply, "Hey, Hy, I thought you were a good friend of mine." I'm sure this is what would have happened because it happened before in the past and it happened subsequently. Despite my advice, historical advice as much as political, Wendell Anderson decided to do that silly thing.

In any case, Lola and Rudy were having lunch in my house. In fact, we sat in the living room rather than the dining room, because Rudy had a lot of papers he wanted to put in front of me. and in the course of the conversation he said, "I need help." Actually, his words, almost verbatim, were, "I don't trust the sons of bitches I have around me now. They are all out for themselves." He said he didn't trust the Anderson group, either.

Then he said that, in order to help him, it would be best if I took a leave from the University and became his chief of staff.

"Oh, that's not going to work," I said.

"Why don't you think it will work?"

"I'm not a chief of staff kind of person."

"What do you mean?"

"I don't give a damn what's going on in the details of stuff."

I said it wouldn't work for another reason. "You and I are friends and have been friends for a long time. You and I are friends in such a way that we are very frank with each other. When you do something I think is crazy, I tell you, and when you see me do something crazy, you tell me, and we respect each other that way. And you are governor. If I worked for you and came to your office and said, 'Rudy, you're full of shit,' what are you going to say? 'You're fired'? I know your temper, Rudy. That's what you'd say."

He thought for a few minutes and said, "You know, Hy, you are absolutely right."

So I never had a title, never had a formal function, but I worked in every aspect of the administration. After a while, when someone would ask what I was doing, Rudy would say, "He is the official historian of the administration," whatever that meant. People were happy with that. I was a professor of history, so officially I was "Official Historian." There is nothing in the table of organization to call for an official historian and official historian isn't on the payroll. So that is how we got around that. My office was right next door to Rudy's. His chief of staff, Terry Montgomery, was across the hall.

Anyway, we're still having lunch and he asked, "Are you going to help?" I say, "Well, what is the first thing you want?" And he says, again, "I have to replace most of those Anderson bastards."

They practically were a different wing of the party. Rudy was of the more progressive wing of the DFL and Wendy Anderson from what was called the pragmatic wing of the DFL. Rudy was the first public official, anywhere in the country, as a state senator in 1964 to come out against the war in Vietnam, before just about anybody. Before there was even a war in Vietnam, he was against it. He took advanced positions all along, all down the line, and this was on his own. It had nothing to do with me. This comes out of what I call Range radicalism, and not out of association with Twin Cities radicalism. In fact, they didn't even understand each other.

But one of the first things Rudy asked me to do was help him write his inaugural address. He said to me, "Hy, I need an inaugural address. You know I can't write too good. Why don't you write it for me?"

I sat down and in an hour I wrote him an inaugural address. I was very quick because I knew what I wanted to do. I said, "We're not going to have any public policies. It's going to be straightforward. Most citizens of Minnesota don't know who the hell Rudy Perpich is. Sure, you're lieutenant governor, but lieutenant governor is like John Nance Garner's definition of a the U.S. vice president's job—it isn't worth a bucket of warm piss."

I figured the first thing he had to do was introduce himself to the people of Minnesota, and how best to introduce himself than by being very personal. Discuss where he came from, where his roots were, what his aspirations were, what he, in fact, felt he represented as the first governor of Eastern European descent. I wrote all of that in.

But Rudy's chief policy aide, Ronnie Brooks, objected. She wanted the inaugural speech to be a kind of catalog of new directions of the administration.

Rudy looked at me and said, "I've got to listen to her," and I said, "OK, listen."

And she wrote him a speech and he couldn't pronounce half the words. So, obviously, he wound up opting for mine. I was very proud of it. It was just two pages long, it lasted about three minutes, and he got a standing ovation. What could be wrong with that?

Here's what I wrote for Rudy:

Mr. Chief Justice, members of the Court, members of the Legislature, distinguished guests and fellow citizens of Minnesota. I wish to express my appreciation to Governor Anderson for his outstanding leadership during the past six years. He has committed himself to making our state a better place to live, to work and to do business.

And to Mary Anderson for the gracious hospitality she has extended to Lola and our family. I welcome [new Lieutenant Governor] Alec and Janice Olson to our partnership in the coming years.

Forty-three years ago I entered kindergarten in a small school on Minnesota's Iron Range. At that time the nation was in the grip of the Great Depression. Millions were unemployed, many were ill-nourished or ill-housed and few had any real economic security. As I entered class that day, my father was unemployed and I spoke no English. And, yet, today, I have taken the oath of office as the 34th Governor of Minnesota. This could not happen in many parts of the world.

For this great honor I owe a debt of gratitude to the people of our state who provided us with an excellent educational system which allowed me, my brothers and others of my generation to achieve the most of which we were capable.

But more importantly I owe a debt to my dedicated parents, Mary and Anton Perpich. My father, an immigrant, was attracted to the United States by the opportunities he envisioned. My parents worked long hours under difficult conditions in order to secure a college education and assure a better way of life for their children. And I am very happy that they can both be here to see their oldest son became the Governor of Minnesota.

It is this dedication, spirit and hard work which I inherited from my parents that I pledge to utilize for the benefit of the people of Minnesota. I pledge to work hard so that present and future generations will have the same opportunities I had and will be able to enjoy the highest quality of life and live a little bit better than ever before.

So, thank you, my fellow Minnesotans for the opportunity to serve you as Governor of this great state.

The inaugural address got good response. Subsequently, I continued to do many things for Rudy. The first major effort I was involved in with him was the state budget. We worked all day and all night putting together that state budget. There was a determination not to give the University any new money, except that Rudy designated one new position for the appointment of a Minnesota historian. Immediately, everyone said, "Ah, Hy is responsible for that." I was shocked.

Then, in the capital budget, he put in funds for the planning of a new University archives building. What happened was that in the course of the first few months of the administration, I took him to the immigrant archives, which was then in an old warehouse. Rudy saw the Croatian collection he was interested in and it was in miserable condition. He came up with a proposal for an archives building. I got into trouble with President Magrath, who figured I was the one responsible for it, but I wasn't, and the U rejected both the Minnesota historian new position and the archives building ideas.

Twenty-five years later, the archives building was built, with the generosity of former governor Elmer Andersen, and it cost fifteen times more than what it would have cost in the 1970s, when Rudy first proposed it.

One action of Rudy's I will take credit for is his statement on history. He was up to that point the only governor I know of who ever issued a formal statement on history. He gave it at historic Fort. Snelling. It called for the funding of the Historical Society and other kinds of initiatives. I'm very proud of having written his speech around that.[1] We came to the realization that the governor's visibility is great, but he has limited opportunities to present new ideas, except through budget messages. We devised a scheme whereby there would be special messages delivered through the legislature. There was a special message on history, a special message on the arts, and a special message on criminal justice.

Here's the way we did it. Take the history speech. A group of interested people would get together in the governor's residence in the basement. For history, we gathered the chairmen of the major history departments in the colleges and the local and state historical societies and had a kind of brainstorming session. We'd pare down the conversation. Rudy would think about what he really wanted out of the message. He'd say, "Okay, it's yours." Then I sat down and wrote the history message. The emphasis of the history message was on ethnicity, class, things of that nature that fitted into his experience, and a message that history should not be a kind of esoteric and upper-class elitist experience but that it was everybody's. That's what I believed, and Rudy agreed.

I spent too many hours at the capitol. Every nonteaching moment

---

1. [The full transcript of this speech is reprinted as "In Conclusion: History through the Eyes of the Vanquished" at the end of this book.—J.W.]

I had was at the capitol. I met my classes, I met my office obligations and my University committee obligations, but every other moment was spent either at the capitol or in the governor's mansion. The State Patrol people, the security guards, every one of them knew me and I knew every one of them. They knew my car. I would drive up to the governor's residence and immediately the gates would open. It was about access to the governor's office and to the mansion. There was one period of forty-eight hours when I didn't leave the mansion because we were working on the budget. All Betty wanted was for me to call every few hours, which I did.

I also offered Perpich political advice. He didn't always want to listen. Take the instance during the summer of 1977 near Hibbing. This was before the start of the gubernatorial campaign. Rudy's birthday party was being held up on the Range, and it was the beginning of fund-raising for the 1978 election too. We were all going up there, but I was mainly heading to the Iron Range because this was the weekend of Johnny Bernard's eighty-fifth birthday.

John Bernard was the U.S. congressman from the Eighth District in northern Minnesota from 1937 to 1939; the Eighth District includes most of the Iron Range. His main claim to fame was that he was the one member of the House of Representatives who voted against a bill that would have banned aid to the democratically elected republican government in the Spanish Civil War. That objection allowed some arms to make it to the anti-Franco, anti-Fascist forces. Bernard's vote alone pretty much ended his electoral career. After he was defeated for re-election, he became a union organizer in northern Minnesota.

It was a celebration of his life up near Hibbing at Mesaba Park, which is the longtime camp of the Finnish Communists. Bernard's party was being chaired by Gus Hall, the general secretary of the U.S. Communist Party. I was on the planning committee, largely because of my role as historian and because they asked me to do it.

Because I was in Hibbing, I stopped by Rudy's family home; Rudy asked me where I was going that afternoon and I told him I was going to Mesaba Park for the Bernard celebration. He said, "I'm coming with you."

"No, you're not."

"What do you mean? I'm the governor."

"They will crucify you."

"They are my people."

Well, Lola understood exactly what I was talking about and she backed me up. "No, Rudy," she said. "You're not going."

He was so stubborn. He was really very stubborn. He insisted that these were his people and Johnny Bernard was a good friend of his. I told him Gus Hall, the Communist leader, was chairing it and he said, "Gus Hall, I've known Gus for a long time." I said, "If the left doesn't crucify you, the right will," and he still couldn't understand. Finally, Lola grabbed the car keys away and told the State Police security, "Don't let him out of the house."

In the meantime, I went quickly out the door and to the meeting, celebration, or rally, whatever you want to call it. Sure enough, the first thing Gus Hall did, in opening up the celebration session, was start an immediate attack on Rudy Perpich. And what did he attack? He challenged Rudy's claim that he was the son of the working class and that his father was an iron ore miner. Hall said there is only one true leader in the world who is a true working-class leader who came out of the iron mines and that is Leonid Brezhnev, general secretary of the Soviet Communist Party, and the crowd applauded.

Can you imagine if Rudy, the governor of the state of Minnesota, were there at that moment? I was sitting there and almost puked. Soon after, I confronted Hall about what he said about Perpich and he responded, "Oh, Professor Berman, I've read a great many things that you've written and I enjoyed and approved of everything you've written."

"Gus," I said, "when I get home, I'm going to have to reread everything to see where I went wrong." All the Communists around him, the yes men, they were ready to shoot me.

Gus Hall didn't particularly care for things I wrote after that.

Wahl and Wellstone

In 1977 President Jimmy Carter appointed Harry MacLaughlin, who had been Walter Mondale's former law partner and was serving as an associate justice of the Minnesota Supreme Court, to be a U.S. district court judge. This gave Rudy an opening to the state supreme court. First, he said, "I don't want fat-cat Republicans, cigar-smoking, big-shot lawyers from the bar association telling me who to appoint." So he established a small committee to help him. It was Bill Kennedy, the Hennepin County public defender, Joe Summers, the Ramsey County judge, and me.

"Rudy, I'm not a lawyer," I said.

"Yeah, that's why I want you to be there, to keep them honest."

There was one other thing he said about the selection: "I want the best candidates' names on my desk. One thing, they all have to be women."

There had never been a woman on the state supreme court. Rudy had promised women's groups that he'd name a woman, and he wanted to make history as he ran for reelection in 1978. We searched and we came up with a list that was very distinguished. I know Esther Tomljanovich was on it, Diana Murphy, Roberta Levy, a few others, and all of them later in life became significant legal people in the state. But I favored Rosalie Wahl right away.

First of all, in my opinion, she was the best overall lawyer. She was a legal scholar. She taught at William Mitchell College of Law. And I knew she developed hands-on teaching there, which I appreciated. She knew the kind of law for practical situations. I think the other guys were leaning toward Roberta Levy, but Wahl won over Rudy and she became a terrific justice.

Around this time, another historic figure emerged. There was an anti–power line struggle going on in parts of Minnesota, with farmers rising up against electric cooperatives who wanted to construct big power towers on their land. That's when I got to know Paul Wellstone. I probably first met him because he was teaching at Carleton College and I was at the University, but I really got to know him when he was running the anti–power line movement and Rudy was governor. Those were power cooperatives he was fighting, and co-ops were part of the DFL coalition.

Rudy asked me, "Do you know this professor at Carleton? Whatever his name is, would you go and speak to him and see if you can get him to calm down a bit? We believe in the protections of farmers' interest and farmers' rights. But these are cooperatives, you know."

So I called Paul to have lunch and we were talking and halfway through, Wellstone said, "Rudy sent you, didn't he?"

"Yeah, he did."

"Tell Rudy to go fuck himself."

That sort of ended the conversation. I went back and told Rudy, "I don't think the guy's going to cooperate." And then, over the years, they became good friends.

In my dual role as university professor and governor's confidant, Rudy often arranged to have someone on his staff drive me. One of those staff people was a young fellow named Mark Dayton. You may have heard of him. It wasn't his regular assignment, but periodically he would drive me. One day in early 1978 we were traveling from the capitol to the University and Mark said to me, "Hy, I'm getting married."

"Congratulations, Mark. Who's the lucky lady?"

"Well, she's a Rockefeller, Alida Rockefeller."

I was sitting right next to him in the passenger seat and I kind of fell silent for a moment. Then I turned to him and said, "Geez, Mark, can't you share the wealth a little bit?"

Ambition and Defeat

In 1978 Rudy had to run for reelection. His elevation to governor was just a two-year thing. It was also a year for a U.S. Senate open seat because of the death of Hubert Humphrey earlier that year. After Hubert's death, his wife, Muriel Humphrey, filled out his term, but she didn't run again, so there was a DFL party primary in which Bob Short and Don Fraser squared off.

And that, to me, is the biggest issue that caused the defeat of Rudy Perpich in the 1978 gubernatorial race.

Fraser was a U.S. congressman and was nominated by the DFL convention. He was challenged by Short, a wealthy businessman and a longtime Northside Minneapolis DFLer. Short owned the Leamington Hotel and the Washington Senators baseball team before it became the Texas Rangers. Not sure what it was about that team that attracted owners I detested. There was Bob Short, on the one hand, and then George W. Bush, on the other, who was the Rangers owner before he became our very bad forty-third president of the United States.

The challenge of Don Fraser split the DFL, of course, and what Short did was rally the right-wing DFL, the anti–gun control, the anti–Boundary Waters Canoe Area Wilderness, and anti-abortion group, a coalition of what I call the Neanderthals, and they defeated Don Fraser in the primary. That was very sad.

Meanwhile, Wendy Anderson had to run, too, for his full term after Rudy appointed him. Anderson also took an anti-BWCAW position. The general antagonism against Anderson for his self-appointment also meant a withdrawal of votes in that contest.

At the same time, Rudy was being challenged by Al Quie, already a distinguished congressman with a distinguished record, who would be retiring from public life and thought the best way of retiring from public life was becoming governor. Rudy was going to win that one, or, it looked like he was going to win it. All the indicators showed him winning, all the polls showed him winning, but the combination of factors—Short's politics, Anderson's selfishness—just doomed Rudy's election.

Specifically, Rudy claimed, and there may be some truth to this, that he lost the election over the last weekend when Minnesota Committee Concerned for Life, the antiabortion group, blanketed the church parking areas of the Twin Cities with leaflets in car windshields saying, "Rudy Perpich Is a Baby Killer." Why? Because Rudy Perpich, at that point, believed in choice, and his brother George was the chair of the Minnesota Senate Health and Welfare Committee, which was a strong blocking point for any antiabortion legislation. And, eventually, his sister-in-law Connie Perpich would be the director of legislative and public affairs for Planned Parenthood in Minnesota and the Dakotas. Now, how much more pro-choice can you get than that? Rudy insisted that his pro-choice stance cost him the election, and that may be true.

I've been to campaign victory celebrations and campaign wakes, if you want to call them that, but the night of the November 1978 election was the worst. It's been called the Minnesota Massacre. Rudy lost. Short lost and Anderson lost. Anderson lost because of ambition and he just didn't have the brains.

It was so bad that we didn't come down from the hotel room. Rudy wasn't with us. He was up north. The hotel was in downtown Minneapolis. We had a suite of rooms. I remember that about midnight, when it was clear that everybody had lost, someone said, "Let's all go have a couple of drinks," and I said, "No, I'm going home." I just went out to my car and went home.

My involvement with Rudy continued after he was defeated. At first, it was figuring out what he could do next. He had given up his license as a dentist and hadn't gone through the continuing education process necessary to keep it. So it would have been difficult to go back into dentistry. Besides, no Republican would trust him with their teeth, and some Democrats wouldn't trust him, either, including me. So becoming a dentist again was not in the cards. And the Humphrey Institute at the University hadn't yet been established as the safe landing place for failed politicians. So there seemed to be no easy place for him to go.

As it turned out, Bill Norris, who was the president and CEO of Control Data, was a good friend of Rudy and thought Rudy had some qualities that would make him valuable as an international representative of Control Data. He convinced Rudy to become vice president of Control Data for international affairs, with headquarters in Vienna. In order to do that, Rudy had to go through training for about six months to a year in New York.

I would periodically see him in New York when I went there for various meetings, and we got together. One night at dinner he asked me what I was doing for breakfast the next morning. I said I was getting up and going to my meetings. He said, "Why don't you get up an hour earlier and I'll come over and have breakfast with you." It was at that breakfast that he told me what he was going to do.

"I will never lose another election," Rudy said. "I will never be defeated again. From now on, you will see a born-again Catholic who has become committed to an antiabortion position. I am no longer a baby killer. I moved away from pro-choice to pro-life."

"Rudy, you can't get away with that. You have a father who is anticlerical and wouldn't be caught dead in a church. In fact, I had trouble having him come to the inaugural mass because he wouldn't go into a church. The only reason I was able to get him to go was that I said, 'Look what that church did to my people and I'm going.' Your father said, 'If you are going to go, I'll go with you.'

"How the hell do you think you can get away with that?" I asked Rudy. He said, "Watch me."

Well, he got away with it—once, in 1982.

He ran against the DFL-endorsed candidate, Warren Spannaus, and he beat Wheelock Whitney in the general election.

Before his return, my contacts with him when he was in Vienna were sporadic. I did not know, though I suspected, that he was going to challenge Spannaus, and not for the DFL endorsement, but for the nomination and the primary. He didn't seek the endorsement. He'd had it with the party. He came back from Vienna and just ran for the primary.

Rudy was angry with me because I supported Spannaus in the endorsement effort. The reason I did was that, first, I had no knowledge he was going to run, and even if he did, I probably still would have supported Warren. This was not because Rudy and I had a falling-out, but just that we disagreed on that fundamental issue of abortion. I couldn't go along with that, so our relationship just moved apart.

In other ways, we parted too. The four years that Rudy was in Vienna moved him perceptibly to the right, and although in the first term, he was to the left of me, now he was to the right of me. I take the view—I told him this—that the relationship between political leaders, business corporations, and labor unions should be cordial but at arm's length. He took the new view that it should be close. If I were a Marxist, or a neo-Marxist, if I were any of that, I'd point to what Marx says, that the government is, in fact, the executive branch of the ruling class. I'm not a Marxist but an unashamed and unabashed liberal, a New Deal liberal at a time when it is unfashionable to be one.

Still, when Rudy became governor for the second time, he asked me to work with him again, but I couldn't bring myself to continue writing messages for him.

One thing we agreed on was his new emphasis on internationalism. This was not only in terms of trade but also in terms of culture and cultural exchange. This was the time when I was going to China periodically. He was intrigued by that, and he was the first Minnesota governor to go to China, largely because I pushed him in that direction. Even though I wasn't in the administration, we still talked.

Then, there came another breaking point. And that was the fallout from the P-9 Hormel strike in Austin, Minnesota, in 1985–86. I was criticized by others on the left for my position on it. I thought the strike at Hormel was a questionable strike, basically an illegal strike. It was a strike of the local, which was a discredited local by its international union. It had no support in the labor movement, and Austin's mayor, who was one of the striking workers, even asked Rudy to call in the National Guard. The only ones who had any kind of enthusiasm for that strike were the New York radicals and some in the Twin Cities, like my

Hy Berman *(left)*, about five years old, with his grandmother, mother, and brother, Harold, circa 1930.

At seventeen, Hy was a counselor at Camp Kinderland, the left-wing, Jewish summer camp that, thirteen years later, got him in the crosshairs of the House Un-American Activities Committee.

Hy was in the U.S. Army from 1943 to 1946, but spent his World War II years on American soil.

The first of his academic achievements: graduation from the City College of New York in 1948.

Hy Berman and Betty Silbering were married in March 1950.

The young Professor Berman as a graduate assistant at Columbia University in the early 1950s.

In 1964 Berman was a University of Minnesota professor traveling the world to teach American studies and labor history—here at Osmania University in Hyderabad, India.

Berman juggled his academic work with being a close adviser to Governor Rudy Perpich and landed where he loved to be: at the intersection of Minnesota politics, history, and public attention. Photograph by Charles Bjorgen; copyright 1977 *Star Tribune*.

Still vibrant at seventy years old, Berman chatted with fellow World War II veterans at a Fort Snelling gathering. Photograph by Richard Sennott; copyright 1995 *Star Tribune*.

Where the professor became the TV personality: through his regular appearances on Twin Cities Public Television's *Almanac* program, Berman solidified his position as Minnesota's premier public historian. Here he engages with hosts Cathy Wurzer and Eric Eskola.

Hy Berman in front of an image of the man he came to know, love, and share a University of Minnesota office with—Hubert Humphrey. Courtesy College of Liberal Arts, University of Minnesota.

friend Peter Rachleff, the Macalester College labor historian. Nobody else had any great enthusiasm.

It was a turning point, no question about it. It was a major loss in terms of the labor movement at the time. But no matter what I felt about the strike, I know I didn't agree with Rudy on his decision in late January 1986 to call out the Minnesota National Guard to help Hormel keep its plant open as it hired scabs to replace striking workers. In some ways, Rudy didn't have a choice, but what he did pretty much put an end to the strike.

A few weeks after the Guard went in, I wrote an op-ed piece in the *Star and Tribune*:

> Hormel strikers in Austin are facing the worst possible problem that confronts unionized employees. Their strike seems to have been broken by a combination of an adamant employer, labor-movement disunity, economic conditions and a hostile political climate on both the state and national levels. . . .
>
> The local union and the strikers did not anticipate management's obstinacy in refusing to budge from industry-wide labor standards, which were sharply reduced by the non-union firms in the industry. Nor did they anticipate that a governor with a long pro-labor record would call out the National Guard. . . .
>
> For all practical purposes the strike is lost.

As I said, I thought the strike was over to begin with, but what I wrote got me into deeper trouble with Rudy. I was told by his staff people that the afternoon after the appearance of my article he received a phone call from his father, Anton, and that the conversation went something like this: "Rudy, you are a strike breaker!"

Remember that Rudy's father was one of the pioneers in trying to organize the iron miners and that he had been blacklisted from the industry for a decade because of it. He was in the left wing of the various formations of William Z. Foster's industrial unionism operations in the 1920s, the Trade Union Unity League and the Trade Union Educational League.

Apparently, Rudy explained carefully and quietly what he had done with the National Guard and why, and his father was quiet through the whole thing. After Rudy stopped, his father said, "Yeah, Rudy, you're my son. I love you dearly, but you are a strike breaker!'" and he hung up with a bang. That didn't exactly endear me with Rudy.

I stand by that article. All I said was historical and factual. When a DFL governor calls out the National Guard to protect scab workers, the strike is over, and that's what he did. Whether he had the justification of doing it or not is another matter. The strike was doomed to begin with, but Rudy's action really put the kibosh on it and on our close friendship.

Finally, he ran again in 1990 and it was that crazy election when Jon Grunseth had to drop out with just weeks to go because of some sort of sex scandal and Arne Carlson snuck in at the last minute and ran against Rudy. I was asked by KSTP, Channel 5, to be a commentator on election night. Well, the early returns started coming in, and it was clear Rudy was going to lose. At about ten fifteen I called the election for Carlson before anyone else in town.

Fifteen minutes after that, over the loud speaker, I heard, "Phone call for Professor Berman." It was Rudy and he was mad. He wanted to know why I said he'd lost. And I said, "Rudy, because you did." He was blaming me because I gave him the bad news. He wouldn't speak to me for two months.

Still, when I think back on the great governors in Minnesota history, I rank Perpich with Floyd Olson. I know I'm biased because of my friendship with Rudy, but that man did more in his term as governor than any governor before or since. I could point to just a whole slew of things, including some I disagreed with, like the Mall of America, for instance. That was his idea. I told Rudy at the time when the Mall developers, the Ghermezian brothers, came through, I said, "If you believe these guys, I've got a bridge in Brooklyn I can sell you." These were charlatans, but they were effective charlatans.

In any case, he became really serious about it. I said, "Rudy, look at it this way. The megamall—that's what we called it back then—the megamall will destroy downtown Minneapolis, all the businesses downtown, and do we want to go that route?" He said, "Oh, no, they'll survive and they'll thrive." Well, he was wrong and I was right on that one, about destroying downtown Minneapolis. But he was right on the overarching impact of the Mall of America. It has a tremendous impact economically to the state. It's a magnet attracting tourists from all over the world.

Then, his idea for an arts high school was a real privilege for the state. That came about in a conversation I had with him. I told him about the High School of Music and Art in New York. I used to go and listen to nice music there when I was at City College.

"There's a high school specifically for music and art?" he said.

"Yes."

"We should have it here, too." He snapped his fingers, and hello, we had an arts high school.

Same for the Center for Victims of Torture. Who would think that Minnesota has a torture center? From all over the world they come here for treatment. Who could have imagined that? Only Rudy.

Then there was, of course, the World Trade Center in St. Paul. It was his idea to use trade as a weapon to increase the economy of the state. The press went crazy. They called him "Stupid Rudy," running all over the world. "Governor Goofy." Well, it was his biggest failure. But he kept on coming up with ideas.

He came back from Vienna with a proposal that the Austrian government was going to give the University of Minnesota an eleventh-century castle that we could convert into an educational institution in Vienna. The University thought it was a damn good idea, and we started working on it. All of a sudden the press wrote, "Rudy is going to get a castle." They made fun of it. They ridiculed it in such a way that we had to drop it.

He wasn't a dreamer. He was a man with ideas, and, yes, some of them were awful. But he had more ideas in a day than most governors have in their entire administration.

This leads to my relationship with Harold Stassen and Elmer Andersen, two Republican good guys. I got to know Stassen as a result of the article on political anti-Semitism in Minnesota that I wrote about the 1938 gubernatorial election. In that article, I said Harold Stassen was the inadvertent beneficiary of the most blatant political anti-Semitism the state had ever faced. I sent him the article way back in 1976, I guess. He called me up. He said he appreciated getting the article, but he had only one objection to the article and that, of course, was me writing that he was the beneficiary of the anti-Semitism. "I fought it," he said.

"Yes I know, Harold. I know you fought it. You fought it by placing one stinking advertisement in the *American Jewish World* newspaper, but that only went to the Jewish community. You didn't go beyond that and share your fighting with anyone else." He laughed. He knew I was right.

Years later, we appeared together on a public panel on the University's campus radio station, KUOM. I can't remember the topic, really, but afterward I invited him to lunch at the Campus Club. By then he was back in the Twin Cities and had no public position whatsoever, but was still a historic figure, after all, a presidential candidate a million times, a signer for the United States of the United Nations Charter, just a wonderful guy. We kept in touch off and on.

A few years later still, on one of the Twin Cities Public Television *Almanac* programs, I called him one of the most innovative Republicans in Minnesota history. He single-handedly took the Republican Party and transformed it from a right-wing nuthouse into a modern party by accepting the role of internationalism as a critical role the party had to face, and by accepting FDR's New Deal reforms as the social base upon which to build. In other words, Stassen was truly conservative, not reactionary.

To me, Stassen is the father of modern Republicanism, and by that I mean good, old-fashioned Republicanism, not the far-right-wing Republicanism we see now. He even had a national impact because his role in Minnesota made possible Eisenhower's challenges to a more right-wing national party. Stassen heard what I said on *Almanac* and he called me and said, "You are the best public relations man I've ever had." I told him, "I'm not your public relations man. If I were, I'd tell you two things, Harold. One, take that goddamn toupee off your head and, two, stop running for the presidency every four years!"

So, then, I was really flattered when he asked me to speak in 2000 at the dedication of the Minnesota Department of Revenue Building that was named for him. I said, "Harold, it's a great honor to do that. But aren't there Republicans who could do it? I'm well known as a DFLer."

"I know, but you're an honest historian and a good friend of mine. I want you to do it."

"OK, but what about the fallout? Look, the Republicans hate me enough."

"Who cares?" Stassen replied.

Here's what I said about him:

It is fitting that we gather today to dedicate this building in the name of Governor Stassen. Harold Stassen, together with Floyd Olson and Hubert Humphrey, were the transforming figures in twentieth-century Minnesota history. He not only assured the transformation of the State into a progressive force in the domestic sphere, but also led the way to moving the State from a frightened porcupine in foreign affairs to embracing its internationalist role. In so doing, Governor Stassen also changed the Minnesota Republican Party into a modern party that embraced its domestic and international obligations.

For two generations, the Republican Party was Harold Stassen's party and a long string of distinguished public servants owe their beginnings to Stassen.

The Great Depression demanded massive governmental reforms that enlarged the role of government in the economic and social life of the nation and the state. These reforms, carried out by the New Deal Democrats in Washington and by the more radical Farmer-Laborites in Minnesota, needed consensus before the specter of social unrest could be lifted from the nation and the State. By accepting these reforms and pledging to carry them forward efficiently and conservatively, Governor Stassen assured domestic tranquility. Furthermore, he went beyond the Farmer-Laborites in introducing effective civil service reforms and guaranteeing labor harmony through a Minnesota version of the Wagner Act.

When Stassen first became Governor in 1939, war clouds were hovering over the world and aggressive Nazism was threatening the security of Europe. Minnesota had a well-deserved reputation for isolationism. Midwestern suspicion of all things European traced its origins to disillusionment with our involvement in the First World War and in the illusion that the oceans would protect us from harm.

Governor Stassen clearly saw the danger of Fascism and Japanese militarism and supported efforts to strengthen our military preparedness and to support internationalist efforts to stop the threats even if it meant participating in war. And, when war came, Harold Stassen left the State Capitol and entered the Navy. He left behind a legacy of a new, revitalized and transformed Republican Party, and a state that was at the forefront of progressive innovation in domestic policy and a deep commitment to our new role in the world.

A distinguished career as diplomat—the last remaining signatory of the United Nations Charter—a university president, cabinet member in the Eisenhower administration, and longtime conscience of our society in political life followed. But it is the accomplishments in our state during the most threatening times of our history for which Harold Stassen will be remembered and for which we today honor him by dedicating this building in his name.

Stassen died less than a year later. I'm so glad I got that chance to honor him.

The other Republican governor I got to know and really like was Elmer Andersen. I got to know him mostly during the course of time he was on the University's Board of Regents, and particularly when he was the board chair from 1972 to 1975. He was a one-time governor and a full-time mensch. Republican to be sure, but a Republican with heart and soul. We then worked together on a joint article for the University alumni magazine about what was wrong with the two major political parties. I wrote about the DFL, of course, and he about the Republicans.

The last time I saw Elmer was just before the presidential election in 2004, when John Kerry, the Democrat, was running against George W. Bush. Actually, Elmer died soon after that election. He called me and said he wanted me to come over to his house. That's when he was living on Lake Johanna in Arden Hills. He actually wanted me to convince his old friend, Tom Swain, who was his chief of staff during his two years as governor, to leave the Republican Party. He said, "I want him to leave the party before they kick him out."

I said, "Elmer, I haven't been to your house in a while. I know roughly where you live. Give me your actual street address." He said, "If you roughly know where I live, you'll know my house."

So I got to the area and, sure enough, I knew his house immediately. This was a pretty conservative area of the Twin Cities. All the houses around there had Bush campaign signs on their lawns. But one had a Kerry sign. That was Elmer's house. In addition, there was a giant sign in his yard. It said, "Support our troops. Bring them home." Elmer again. Just a wonderful man.

7

University Presidents (and a Few Crises)

I worked under seven presidents at the University of Minnesota. Without a doubt, my favorites were O. Meredith Wilson and Mark Yudof. Of course, I've got some opinions about the others.

Wilson was the first president I met, worked with, and who got my career off to a great start by sending me to the Iron Range. He was a pretty decent early American history scholar in his own right. He opened a bunch of doors for me, like meeting Rudy Perpich and understanding Minnesota's immigrant culture.

But what truly made me a fan was the way he handled a major controversy that centered on Mulford Sibley, the Quaker and socialist political science professor. Mulford was a free thinker. Among other things, he had written a piece for the *Minnesota Daily,* the student newspaper, in which he said there was too much conformity on campus. I'm not sure how serious he was, but he said we should have a Communist club, a free love club, and a nudist club, things like that. It was really his way of saying there should be unlimited free speech. And this was in 1964 when the Cold War was raging and just as the student protest movement was beginning to take form around the country. So here was a faculty member egging students on.

A bunch of politicians in St. Paul got all bent out of shape about Mulford and about the University, in general. Of course, that meant that some of the Regents were upset, too, and a number of them asked President Wilson, "What do we have to do to fire Mulford Sibley?" And Wilson said, "Oh, that's very simple. The first thing you do is fire me." That was magnificent. I loved the guy.

After Wilson moved on to Stanford and a think tank, here came Malcolm Moos. You know how I feel about him when it came to the takeover of his office by the black students. He was missing in action then and on some other critical occasions too. But we got along OK. He's the only president who ever invited me to sit in the president's box during a football game, you know. And he even tried to explain football to Betty, who didn't know a thing about it.

During the Moos years I was involved in trying to organize a faculty union. It came at a time of the first major post–World War II economic downturn, and the University was faced with a number of economic crises. Moos decided to resolve these crises by what he called the two Rs: retrenchment and reallocation. It was the first of a series of steps that led to the erosion of the economic status of the faculty. Compensation began to decline. There were increasing efforts to make the Faculty Senate less meaningful and to move away from what had been a tradition of shared academic governance.

A number of us were convinced that this was a good time to start at least a discussion of faculty unionization. The American Association of University Professors, or AAUP, which had been pretty strong on campus in the 1960s, had become a minimal presence on campus. My colleague and partner in crime, philosopher Burnham Terrell, and a few others got together to talk about the necessity of having some kind of faculty organization. We were joined by a physics professor who—at that time—we didn't know really well, although he'd gone to City College in New York about the same time I did. His name was Erwin Marquit, and, as you know, he and I would go on to have a contentious personal history.

With my contacts in the labor movement, I quickly became enmeshed with the American Federation of Teachers. We formally established a University of Minnesota Federation of Teachers group with the objective of achieving a collective bargaining agreement. We had a significant support base that led us to believe that we would, if not be successful, at least would come close. We went through the process. We quickly gathered enough membership cards to trigger a union election. Obviously, an opposition group immediately arose. That opposition group was what had once been the AAUP and was a group of faculty members that was very close to the administration, many of whom became administrators very soon after the end of this campaign. They were backed by the Moos administration, which blocked our usage of campus mail to communicate with faculty in our organizing effort. This was before email, of course, so it was easy to hinder communications. My History Department colleague, Paul Murphy, was one of the leaders of the opposition.

So I'm the president of this outfit, Terrell is vice president, and Marquit is secretary-treasurer, and we're gaining some steam. But in the midst of all this, Marquit announces that he is going to run for governor at the head of the Communist Party ticket. When I heard that, my immediate thought was, "There go our union efforts." When a *Daily* reporter contacted me he asked whether Marquit's CP candidacy was going to hurt or help our election campaign. My response—glib but meaningful—was something like, "It would help only if Paul Murphy announced that he had become a member of the American Nazi Party."

The reporter, of course, printed that, and for a long time, as you might suppose, it alienated me from both Murphy and Marquit.

Marquit thought I was red-baiting him, but how anybody could be a Stalinist in the 1970s, well, I question his political judgment if not his moral stance, but that's beside the point.

The election took place and we were overwhelmingly defeated, at which point I resigned as president, and faculty union supporters became a sect, rather than an organized group. Two things became clear. First of all, that unionization was not what the majority of the faculty wanted and I wasn't about to push anything that the majority of the faculty didn't want. Or, to put it another way, I kept telling my colleagues that I was beginning to get sick and tired of doing social work for the affluent. I was being facetious in that, but that's how it felt.

The other thing that bothered me was that the American Federation of Teachers was, in fact—and this is what bothered me most—spending dues money of elementary and secondary school teachers who were not as well paid, not as well treated as University faculty, to organize University faculty. If they were doing that for the purpose of organizing teaching assistants or something like that, it might have been justifiable. But for us privileged Ph.D. faculty? That wasn't right.

The hiring process that led to C. Peter Magrath's appointment in 1974 was, for me, a real scandal. The top candidate was David Saxon, who would later become president of the University of California system. Saxon was of the Saxon Ford family, a St. Paulite. So he was a local and Jewish, and this is 1974. One of the Regents on the search committee was L. J. Lee, from Bagley, Minnesota. During the search, Lee admitted he asked Saxon about his religion and if he belonged to any religious group. He later said he didn't want an agnostic to lead the University of Minnesota. I think he meant he didn't want a Jew.

At the early point of the search no one seemed to know this sort of questioning had occurred. But one of the other Regents, George Rauenhorst, a man with decent sensitivities but very little brains, came knocking on my office door and said, "Hy, you won't believe this," and he told me what was going on. George came from a prominent Catholic family. My first thought was, "Jesus, George is a little bit nuts. He couldn't have gotten this right." So I checked with the then-acting academic vice president, Hal Chase, a political scientist, a guy who defended the war in Vietnam and debated me on it, but we were very good friends nonetheless. By the way, Hal Chase was Jewish and he was at that point, I think, the only Jewish reserve brigadier general in the Marine Corps.

When I told Hal what Rauenhorst had told me, he said, "I'm afraid George was right. That's what happened." And I said, "Well, screw this." I picked up the phone and called a couple of reporters I knew at the *Star* and the *Tribune*. There were two newspapers then. And pretty quickly it became big headlines. By then, Saxon had dropped out. He didn't want to work someplace that had a religious test.

Magrath got the job and there were legislative hearings to look into Lee's questions. He wound up getting away with it. The Jewish community was up in arms, as it should have been. It was just another reminder of lingering anti-Semitism in Minnesota. But one of the outcomes of it all was that the legislature the next year elected two Jews to the Board of Regents, Erwin Goldfine from Duluth and Bob Latz from Minneapolis.

Ken Keller, who also happened to be Jewish, came after Magrath and, in my opinion, he was the closest to what our ideal of a president should be. He was a brilliant academic who was completely concerned about academic matters. For example, he had little interest in athletics, although, like all of them, he had his share of scandals. They're hard to avoid.

I was supportive of his "Commitment to Focus" plan, which was, really, to make the University more selective and competitive, but I understood the opposition to it too. I know Keller was criticized for being elitist, because one of the elements was to do away with remedial education and General College, which eventually happened under President Bob Bruininks about twenty years later. So Keller was ahead of his time. But since the expansion of the community college system in the state of Minnesota, particularly in the Twin Cities area, there's really no need for a General College anymore. I know that's not popular to say, but it's true.

Actually, I think it was Rudy Perpich who gave Keller the "Commitment to Focus" idea. I remember one session where Ken was sitting with Rudy. Rudy said the problem with the University is that it tries to be all things to all people. "Whatcha gotta do," he said, and that's how he spoke, "whatcha gotta do is commit yourself to focus." This was to focus the University in certain areas. That's what Keller tried, and I thought he was doing a wonderful job, but he was damaged by a scandal of spending too much money renovating Eastcliff, and, to me, it was a made-up scandal.

It was created by the newspapers and by one of the Regents, Charles McGuiggan. It was McGuiggan's goal, and a few other Regents, to get rid of Keller, frankly, because he was a New York Jew and they couldn't stand him. He was too smart for them. Half the time they couldn't understand what he was saying. But he wasn't a great manager or a great delegator. That hurt him with the Regents and at the legislature.

In the end, Keller was a victim of change and was brought down by the clash between his vision of excellence and the populist, democratic traditions of our state. The University had suffered through a decade of retrenchments and reallocations. One consequence was the relative decline of the University as many of our peer institutions caught up with, and even overtook, us in the national ratings. Keller wanted to reverse that trend with his Commitment to Focus. He thought we had to up our game for undergraduates by slowly reducing enrollment and improving the undergraduate experience. He wanted us, too, to return to being a top-notch research university. His legacy can't be dismissed. New faculty chairs were created by Keller's fund-raising efforts and, more importantly, there was a reconsideration of the goals and objectives of the University.

Minnesotans are willing to put up with many things at the U, including losing football and basketball teams, but they are not willing to comprehend limiting access to the University or excessive hubris on the part of its leadership. That was Ken's demise. The public wasn't educated on the need for change at the U, and the spending scandal confirmed our elitist tendencies. Ken lasted three years, and that was very disappointing. He would have been a great one for a long time.

This leads to my experience in what I call the "tenure war." It occurred when Nils Hasselmo was president. I'd known Nils for a long time. We met when he was hired as an assistant professor of Scandinavian languages and literature. I was then director of the Social Sciences program. He came to my office to talk about how he had some ideas about working with languages and linguistics, and about putting together a course on second-generation retention of languages. I thought it was great because I had a good friend, Joshua Fishman, who did similar work around Yiddish, first at the University of Pennsylvania and later in Israel. So we got along.

Then Nils went up the administrative ladder, chair of the department, then associate dean, then academic vice president, all the rungs. He jumped to the University of Arizona for a few years. After Keller resigned, the Regents were looking for someone who seemed more Minnesotan, and you can't get more Minnesotan than a Swede named Nils. The other candidate for the job was Bob Stein, the dean of the Law School. All of my academic friends in the disciplines wanted Nils because he was one of them. I supported Stein, not because I disliked Nils, but because I thought Stein, although in a professional school, had a better sense of what the University needed and had a more forceful personality. Nils probably heard that I was backing someone else, because he and I never continued our friendship when he was president. As a matter of fact, it broke when I took the lead in the battle of the tenure wars.

This was an attempt by some of the Regents to, in my opinion, do away with tenure as we knew it, and it also almost resulted in the revival of a faculty union, which had failed earlier. Regent Jean Keffeler was the spearhead of the effort to change the tenure code. Ironically, she was put forward as a Regent's candidate by my good friend and colleague Allan Spear, who had gone on to become a Minnesota state senator. Spear told me he put Keffeler forward because she was intelligent, liberal, and a DFLer. I beg to differ on two of those descriptions.

The ostensible reason the Regents tried to change the tenure code had to do with our Medical School and all of the Academic Health Sciences. The provost of our AHC, William Brody, found himself in a big dilemma. The AHC had used soft money to make hard hires, believing that soft money would always come in from patient fees and things like that. But somehow or other the health of Minnesotans was such that there was a sharp downturn in patient fees, so he was stuck with a budget he couldn't meet, and the only way to meet it was to get rid of ten faculty members. He called it "restructuring." We called it an attack on tenure. So, a particular need of the Medical School was translated into a broader policy initiative on faculty tenure.

Hasselmo had been a faculty member and knew that this was going to be a big thing, but he failed to stop the Regents from going after tenure. I fault him for that. It was a massive uprising and it rocked the campus for a good year, and I was in the middle of that.

I knew instinctively that Keffeler didn't know the culture of the University. I met her at the Campus Club, with a number of other people there. She was then chair of the board and I said, "Jean, I would be willing, and I'm sure some of my colleagues in the History Department would be willing, to sit down with you and any number of the members of the Board of Regents to give you a kind of background of the historical culture of this university. I think you don't understand it."

She responded by saying, "I'm not interested in learning history. I'm interested in making history."

Well, that was the end of that conversation until Doug Grow, the columnist for the *Star Tribune,* went to a meeting of a group of us who were planning the next step in the tenure wars. I told him the story about Keffeler and her wanting to make history by destroying tenure, and he wrote a brutal column about Keffeler, saying she was a management type who disregarded people and that she was chasing away good faculty to other universities like Wisconsin and Michigan.

Keffeler called me up and denied ever saying that. I said, "Well, you can deny all you want, but there are witnesses that you said it." A couple of months later, she resigned from the board. Tenure was saved, but I think that was the low point in my experience as a faculty member in all the years I was involved in faculty governance.

I loved Mark Yudof. Mark and I had a great friendship and it began even before he was officially hired.

The chair of the search committee in 1997 was an old friend of mine from the Rudy Perpich administration, Jerry Christenson. Great guy, but, honestly, not very Jewish. Jerry called me up and said a final candidate was the provost from the University of Texas and he happened to be a very observant Jew. Jerry wanted me to help integrate Yudof into the Jewish community. I said, "Fine with me."

So the first time I met Mark was at Morrill Hall, the University's administration building. He was there for interviews, and I told him about the vibrancy of the Jewish community, and the fact that it's so diverse, with so many active synagogues. I had learned that his wife, Judy, was a leader of the Conservative Jewish movement, and she knew that we have very strong Conservative congregations in Temple of Aaron, Adath Jeshurun, and Beth El. Then I gave him my little book, *Jews in Minnesota*. Maybe that sealed the deal for him to come, who knows?

The next contact I had with him was when he had accepted the position, and Bob Bergdahl was in town. This was in 1997. Bob was the president of the University of Texas—Mark's boss, really—and he had gotten his doctorate at the U in German history a few years after I arrived. He was one of my students, and the guy's the president of a great university and was back in Minneapolis getting an honorary degree, and his provost, Yudof, was becoming Minnesota's president. A big deal.

Anyway, Hasselmo invited Betty and me to Eastcliff for dinner to celebrate Bob's arrival. I was not on Hasselmo's invite list. I was on Bergdahl's list. I didn't know that at the time but learned later, and I'll tell you why in a minute.

At the dinner I was seated next to Yudof. Must have been the Jewish table. Bergdahl came from South Dakota and I'm guessing a big Norwegian family because Eastcliff was filled that night with a bunch of Scandinavians—including Hasselmo—except for Yudof and me. Yudof was looking around—and it kind of went quiet in the room—and he said to me, "Is it always like this?" And I said, as quietly as I could, "Yes." But he said so too many people could hear, "That's too bad!"

Then Yudof compared it to Texas and said, "I'm gonna like it here. I mean, this president's house is just five blocks from a kosher butcher shop. In Austin I have to go all the way to Chicago to get kosher food."

Anyway, after that, we were having a very nice time when Bergdahl got up and gave his talk, thanking everybody in the room, and he got to me. "And, finally, I want to thank Hy Berman, who was my first professor. I was his teaching assistant and he taught me how to exploit students." That was the reason I was invited, so he could make that comment. And I laughed, I laughed hard. He knew damn well I didn't exploit students and I never thought about doing that.

The irony of the night was that Yudof wanted to be president of the University of Texas but figured he wouldn't get the job because Bergdahl would be there forever. No sooner did he accept the Minnesota job but a few months later Bergdahl accepted the chancellor's job at Berkeley and left Texas altogether.

Yudof was a very, very committed Jew, you know. Very committed. He decided that what he wanted to do was to reestablish an old tradition that began at the University of Chicago, and there should be a substantial debate over a very significant issue: what's better, the latke or the hamantashen? For the Gentiles out there, a latke is a potato pancake that Jews eat at various holidays but, mostly, at Hanukkah. And a hamantashen is a three-cornered pastry that Jews eat during the holiday of Purim. Haman is the bad guy in the book of Esther who drives the story.

It was the classic latke-hamantashen debate. Sort of like Lincoln and Douglas. At the University of Chicago, it started way back in the 1940s and was a scholarly debate with all kinds of footnotes, but, of course, halfhearted. Yudof decided to revive it. A group of professors was selected to take sides in this battle—one of them happened to be Ken Keller, and we've already talked about him—and Yudof was going to be the moderator and the judge. He's a lawyer, you know. By then, he'd already gotten a reputation as a pancake lover. It was a brilliant PR move, the new president of the University traveling around the state testing the best pancakes. The guy just loved pancakes.

So, as the latke-hamantashen debate began, Yudof started to introduce everybody and I stood up. "I have a real problem," I said. "Point of order, Mr. Chairman! Point of order! I demand that you recuse yourself on the grounds of prejudice and bias. We all know that the pancake is the first cousin of the latke, and your love of pancakes is well known. You, sir, are biased. Your prejudices are clear. I demand that you recuse yourself."

Well, he was taken aback for a moment and then he said, "Professor Berman, I will not recuse myself. I am using the power of the presidency. I'm the president. Sit down." And I said, "I bow to power, not to wisdom." The debate ended with everybody getting a latke and a hamantashen, so all's well that ends well, I guess.

That ribbing between the two of us was at the center of our relationship. Soon after the latke argument, I was sitting at the Campus Club in the middle of some kind of a sports crisis, one of our many basketball scandals. I forget which one. He came over looking serious and sat down at my table. I was ready to advise the president of the University. He said, "Hy, I have a serious question to ask you." I said, "Whatever you need." He asked, "How much basketball eligibility do you have left?" I don't think I've ever dribbled a ball in my life, but we laughed and laughed.

By the way, we had one interaction that I'm very thankful for. He came to a gathering of some of my faculty pals one night and I casually told him, "I think I'm going to retire at the end of this year." That would have been 1999, and I was already seventy-four years old. He said, "Don't you dare. I need you around here. This place won't be the same without you." He told me about this thing called phased retirement. I didn't know anything about phased retirement. He said, "Take that, you'll be here for five years on a reduced schedule and you get benefits." It sounded too good to be true, so I said, "Sure, I'll apply for that." I got it, so I stayed five more years. In other words, I would have retired five years earlier if it weren't for Mark Yudof. And he left before I retired.

He was a very good president and the calming spirit after the storm of the Hasselmo presidency, which had lasted about a decade. First, he raised a billion dollars, something the University never could do before. Second, he came on campus and said, "This place is ugly. It's terrible. Dirty, filthy, unkempt." He cleaned it up. It's a beautiful campus now. As an academic you don't usually take pride in stuff like that, but it was an achievement, a big achievement.

8

Life as a Public Historian
The *Almanac* Years

My career at the University was capped in 2002 when I received its Outstanding Community Service Award for being Minnesota's premier public historian. I got an award as well as a salary supplement, which lasted as long as I was still teaching. It was a fitting punctuation mark on my career.

To begin with, I always believed that a historian's role is not only to discover new facts, get new interpretations, and bring new scholarship to bear on important historical problems, but also to make that material readily available to ordinary people. Probably my populist approach to things went back to my political orientation and my desire to be a people's historian.

Even when I was first starting, when I was in City College of New York and Brooklyn College, even before I got my doctorate, I was called periodically by WNYC, which is the New York City public radio station, to appear on programs to integrate history into public events, and I remember doing that with a degree of satisfaction. I didn't do it that often in New York because of who I was—a graduate student and beginning instructor—but, nonetheless, they called on me periodically, so I got a taste of that.

At Brooklyn College I remember John Hope Franklin, then chair of the History Department, after hearing me on the radio saying, "You've got a talent for it, Hy. You should cultivate it." When this great historian tells me I should cultivate it, I thought I should, and I have.

When I got here to Minnesota, public television then was called Educational Television. Channel 2 was a medium without a message. It was looking for things. They came to the History Department in search of someone to conduct shows on American history, but there was nobody who was interested in doing that. Most of my colleagues in U.S. history were kind of camera shy. So it fell to me, and I organized the first television course on U.S. history for Channel 2, and maybe for any TV station.

It was very difficult. All the visuals had to be carted from the University right to the studio. The Channel 2 studio was out on Como Avenue, right across the street from the State Fairgrounds. A lot of the visuals I wanted to bring were framed with glass. It was heavy stuff. I was told by the staff of Channel 2 that it was one of the most watched programs of the week. By that they meant they had three or four people watching it.

I tried to be interactive, but unfortunately, interactive in the early 1970s meant writing letters. There was no such thing as email or telephone calls. There was a tape recording machine they used. I got people calling in questions or comments, and if I had two or three in the week I thought, my God, it's really successful.

Once, I invited a barrage of calls, like six or eight messages. It had to do with the late nineteenth-century Indian wars. It started with the Dakota uprising in Minnesota. I did an interpretation of it, which, apparently, most of the people watching Channel 2 had heard for the first time, which was an interpretation based on the point of view of the victim rather than the victor. The messages said, "We don't want your interpretations. We want only the facts."

I decided I would follow that. The next show I said, "I'm going to give you a lecture of only facts and—when you wake up—you'll decide that you want more than just the facts." I went through kind of a dry presentation, and the producer in the studio started shouting. "You're putting everybody to sleep," to which my response was, "That's exactly my point!" I continued with my interpretations, but this notion of "just the facts" gave me an opportunity for the next program to start with, "What is historical fact?"

I was able to use, on-screen, an illustration of facts that are not facts, and facts that are counterfacts, and facts that could be facts, and facts that are dependent upon interpretive claims. That was my first experience in truly electronic public history, and I really did enjoy it, although it was a lot of work. Periodically, Minnesota Public Radio, which was also in its infancy, would call me regarding historical background around current events.

At some point, Channel 2 moved from educational to public television, and it began to be more sophisticated in its programming. That's when *Masterpiece Theatre* became a national phenomenon. Public television saw itself not just as talking heads but as something more than just educational. At that point, public affairs programming became very important. The first public affairs program that Channel 2 put together was hosted by a policy wonk by the name of Ted Kolderie.

Ted was a very bright guy, but very dull, and they needed to beef it up. They asked me to appear on the program with him because they knew every time I'd appear I would make some kind of statement that would stir things up. I started getting invitations to come to this periodically. But Kolderie's pubic affairs program was, in fact, in the final analysis, a failure because it didn't attract a lot of viewers and it was too wonkish in its approach.

The design of what later became *Almanac* was what really created an opportunity for me to work as part of a team that would integrate history into public affairs and public events. *Almanac,* which is probably the most successful public affairs program of any public television channel in the United States, was started in 1984. The first host of it was my fellow insider in the Perpich administration, Judge Joe Summers. Joe and Jan Smaby were the original hosts. They asked me to appear on the very first program, and in the course of its decades of existence, I've been appearing on it throughout. I might be the person who's been a guest the most.

A real highlight of my *Almanac* appearances was the creation of five programs of the five most important events in Minnesota history in the twentieth century, which reached its crescendo with the most important event of the century presented at a fifteenth-anniversary celebration of *Almanac.* Governor Jesse Ventura was there, and that was when I had my infamous contact with him.

I had already named four other key moments in the state's history. They were the 1934 Teamsters' strike that galvanized the labor movement and saw tremendous police misconduct. There was Governor Harold Stassen's role and commitment to internationalism, which differentiated us from other states. There was Minnesota's role in the rise of the American shopping mall, what with Southdale and the Mall of America being groundbreaking innovations. A little bit offbeat, I know, but very important in our national identity. And fourth was our penchant for third-party candidates and movements.

Now, it was my opportunity to cite the event in the century that represented the best of Minnesota and our impact. I selected Hubert Humphrey's approach to human and civil rights, which emerged out of the anti-Semitic climate in Minneapolis and his efforts to fight it. Before the show that night when I was going to present my opinion, I walked into what's called the green room where they make you up. Governor Ventura came bounding in, sat down next to me, and said, "Hey, Professor, I hear you're going to tell us the most important event in Minnesota history in the twentieth century, is that right?"

"Yes."

"I can't stick around for it. Can you tell me now?"

"Sorry, Governor, but the producers asked me to keep it quiet until I present it on the air."

"Oh, come on, you can tell me. I'm the governor."

"I'm sorry, I can't."

"You don't have to tell me. I know what it is. My election to be governor of Minnesota."

"Oh, Governor Ventura," I said. "I'm sorry to disabuse you, but it wasn't that. But, OK, because you are governor, I'll tell you. The most important event in Minnesota history in the twentieth century was my appointment to the University of Minnesota faculty."

I didn't know if Jesse was going to sock me or what. He looked so angry, and finally he burst out laughing. So I told him my real belief that it was Humphrey's stand on human and civil rights. His response was, "Oh, guys like you perpetuate difficulties within the society. You're the ones who want forced busing and stuff like that."

Well, that was his attitude, but public history is based on different views. Besides my media appearances, I also was involved in creating what's now called National History Day in Minnesota and, of course, I was active in the Minnesota Historical Society and the American Association for State and Local History. My colleagues in the History Department in the 1970s and '80s didn't see public history as an important aspect of our profession and they really looked down upon it. In fact, I would say their hostility was very great.

But I never got the feeling that I was overcommitted to public history at the expense of doing the kinds of things some of my colleagues were doing. I was still publishing articles, doing research, and appearing on panels at history conferences and seminars. I didn't publish as many books as probably I should have, but I don't regret it at all. I helped make TV documentaries. I was on *Almanac,* what, a hundred times? In the absence of public history in Minnesota, I thought that was a role I had to play. So there's one less book gathering dust on the shelves. So what?

As for the classroom, in preparing students for citizenship in the twenty-first century, I always thought the University owes the students a sense of place and a sense of time.[1] I think it owes the students an opportunity to give them a sense of location, where they are in their culture and in their society. In order to do that, I think it's absolutely essential that students are at least made acquainted with the history of our country, the diverse character of our society, the problems of contemporary living, and the United States in the world. I think students also have to be capable of using tools of communication, language, language expression—oral, written—and also mathematical. I think the University is striving to do it. I think it succeeds more often than it fails.

People also have often asked what do I feel are the key lessons or insights that I wanted to deliver to my students or have them leave with from my class. Well, I don't think that there is a set of key insights I would want my students to have. What I would like them to have is, perhaps, an approach—if you want to be fancy—about the methodology. What I'd like them to have is the ability to see the present in terms of the development of their own society's past, to be able to have some kind of understanding that the world didn't begin with their birth, and that the problems they face have been cumulative and the society in which they live has been cumulative. And what I like for them to come away with is an idea that there is a necessity to look into the experience

---

1. [Much of this is excerpted from Berman's interview on *Portrait,* KTCA-TV, October 15, 1991.—J.W.]

of the past in order to understand their own contemporary world and their own situation in that contemporary world. That's what I like them to come away with.

Because I didn't go into the classroom with a view that I knew exactly what happened. I don't. Nor did I want to go into the classroom with the certitude of a definitive theoretical construct about where we are and how we got here. What I like them to come away with is the ability to think critically by using historical materials in order to understand their present condition.

Now, certainly I had a point of view and it wasn't hidden from the students, but it wasn't presented as the truth with a capital T. Rather, it was presented as an approach that may be right, probably is right, because I'm saying it. But it could also be wrong.

Looking back, over the years, in a way, I think, I've become more tolerant. At one time, I thought that, you know, there was a direction in which society must go in order for the good life to be achieved for most people.

I am not quite so sure anymore. Why? Perhaps all my previous sacred cows have turned out to be nothing but donkeys. Let's take my generation's, or my left-wing generation's, attraction to socialism. What has that turned out to be in practice? It's turned out to be another kind of excuse for centralized state oppression. We didn't view socialism in these terms. We saw socialism as liberating, as freeing, not constraining.

What happened? It got into the wrong hands, but it got into the wrong hands for the ideological reason that socialism is the statist intermediary between the class oppression of capitalism and the total freedom of communism. And as such, it became Stalinized, if you wish, and, for all practical purposes, it makes no difference whether it was Stalinized or Trotsky-ized or Mao-ized; it would have been one of these "izes."

I became more open to alternative views. That doesn't mean I'm accepting the inequalities of the oppression of capitalist societies. Don't get me wrong. I didn't move into the camp of the celebrators, that is, the mindless celebrators of capitalism. There's something to celebrate, but I'm not going to be a mindless celebrator.

I think over the years, I've become much broader in my approach to things, partially through my lecture experiences in China, Germany, Poland, the Netherlands, and India, to name a few.

Trying to deal with students in these different international settings, with subject matter similar to what I was doing here at the University of Minnesota, gave me a kind of insight into a thinking of people who come out of different cultures and historical traditions. Plus, the fact that I was able to live and immerse myself in these societies, in China, Germany, Poland, et cetera. So that also had an impact.

I found myself being more appreciative of national cultural differences, and, therefore, national cultural approaches to common problems. It fits into me becoming more tolerant and open, and much more willing to accept diverse approaches, and much more intolerant of intolerance.

I've also thought a lot about teaching. I know online education is here and it's going to be here, but what its overall value is, I don't know, because, really, education, learning, is about human interaction. Yes, you can get information online and you can absorb information online, but what you do with it depends on your interaction with other people, with a professor or a teacher or other students.

Early on, many years ago, maybe the 1990s, I was involved in doing advanced technological stuff. I gave a course that went over the air to the University's different campuses, sort of closed circuit, I guess. But I insisted that the sessions be devoted to being interactive. We had the possibility of talking to the students in different cities, and them talking to me. I think that's the essence of the teaching and learning experiences.

I've also thought a lot about the conflict today that exists between the hard sciences and the social sciences and humanities, and the belief, I think, on the part of a lot of people in the humanities, and some of the social sciences, is that the money goes to engineering, the money goes to health sciences, and that the university has become more of a trade school. The point is that the money flows where the market is in this capitalist society. Unfortunately, the market is in the sciences and technology, not in the humanities and, to a lesser extent, the social sciences. If you go by the values of the marketplace, the university is doing what the marketplace demands.

Is this right? Is it just? No, it's not right or just. It is an aspect of the university that bothers me. It became a credentialing institution. It had always been the credentialing institution, but since the '70s it has become essentially the institution that gives credentials as a pass to employment.

When I was getting my degrees, the sciences still had the larger share of the university budget, no question about that. They demanded a larger share because we in the social sciences and humanities had no labs and facilities like that. That's part of it. The other part, of course, is that as the university became much more interested in problem solving and research for industry, the sciences and medical science became much more important. It was economics, but politics, of course, follows economics.

It comes down to progress. After all, we believe in progress, don't we? I can get progress by doing fundamental research or I can get progress by doing applied research. We get progress with applied research, so applied research was much more valued than fundamental research. Pure science was sort of downplayed. Actually, I think I benefited from this approach, because I believe, essentially, in applied research. I have always preferred to translate history to help people understand what's going on today. And I've been resented for that by others in the University the way hard scientists resent English professors and archaeology professors. They say, "Look at him, he's on *Almanac* again talking to people instead of writing another book that only three people will read." That's what they say or, at least, think. That, of course, is one of the banes of higher education, the kind of tendency of a discipline to become narrower and narrower, particularly in the humanities and social sciences. It seems these days the narrower the better. It's now valued scholarly work to know more and more about less and less. It drives me crazy. But the great ones research and write in broad strokes, like Allan Nevins on a full history of the United States or Salo Baron on the social and religious history of the Jews from the beginning of time to the present.

My God, that's real scholarship. Now, the great thing is to write about Lincoln's left foot, or every little detail.

These things that annoyed me weren't the reason I decided to retire when I was seventy-five. I thought it was a good time. I thought that's a symbolic time. Who wants to go on beyond that? My classes were still well attended. As a matter of fact, I was accelerating during those years. But then President Yudof talked to me about that phaseout program at the U. As I phased out, I taught half-time, but I did more *Almanac* appearances than ever. I did a couple of documentaries. I wrote a couple of articles and op-eds. I wasn't slowing down at all, absolutely not. If Yudof hadn't told me about that phaseout, I would have simply retired. But I lasted four more years, until I was seventy-nine. I read things I never thought I would read, but I really got into watching operas on DVD. I kept professionally active as well, by participating in symposiums and meetings, and giving lectures periodically. I really enjoyed it, but I know others who couldn't do it. As a matter of fact, a couple of my colleagues who retired, a few months after they retired they just dropped dead. I don't know why.

As for me being on *Almanac,* being interviewed on MPR, and analyzing returns in TV on election night, that kept me active and engaged. It's what I believed in because public history is an obligation we historians have, particularly if we teach in land-grant institutions, which, by their very nature, have as their objective to be people's universities. We're supposed to reach out to our communities. If we do not do that, then I think we are shirking one of the most important elements of our role as historians. I saw my job as translating the best and most accurate historical knowledge regarding the state, the nation, and the society for the public at large. I think I was reasonably successful at that.

Actually, that public role enhanced my life and satisfaction as a University of Minnesota professor, which was really fun. I mean, where else can you constantly be involved in meeting students fresh and new and always having an opportunity to interact with them? Where else can you have a chance to raise questions regarding your own specialty and have it challenged by graduate students, and have the exchanges that lead, I hope, to some form of deeper knowledge and deeper understanding?

IN CONCLUSION
History through the
Eyes of the Vanquished

My concern and interest in our history is long and deep. I have seen an immigrant generation and their children become productive and contributing Minnesotans. I have seen their struggle to maintain their own heritage, and place it alongside the cultures of other ethnic groups to create a genuine American society.

I have experienced and deeply felt the need of immigrants and of my own generation not to be shunned, nor swallowed up by an earlier established culture.

I have seen and participated in movements for the inclusion of all human experience into our historical record and have come to appreciate the need for constant re-evaluation and openness.

History is not only a classroom or archives exercise, or a subject taught by the coach. It is not the sole possession of the super patriot or of the intellectual. We all are a part of history and history is a part of us.

The struggles of our ancestors, the sacrifices they made to achieve a better life for all of us, should have prepared us long ago to expect that newer groups in our society would make similar demands and with the same justice. Exclusionary policy leads to divisiveness, disunity, and disorder.

A better understanding of our past would have cushioned the stresses

[This is a transcript of "Policy Speech on Minnesota History and Heritage," written by Hy Berman and delivered on April 15, 1977, by Minnesota governor Rudy Perpich. Hy had encouraged the governor to give this address on the importance of public history, and he told me numerous times how proud he was of it.—J.W.]

of the last decade when women, minorities, and the young insisted upon their rights to be fully included in our culture. But the lessons of history are learned only when knowledge becomes a familiar part of our daily lives and thoughts.

For the last few years I have been able to put my feelings into constructive action as the state's chairperson for the Bicentennial. I have traveled the length and breadth of our state and have seen and felt the thirst for participation in our history, expressed by young and old both, in rural and urban sections of Minnesota.

Long before *Roots* appeared in a book and on television, demonstrating the hunger of our black citizens to learn about their heritage, I sensed the same hunger among all segments of our state's population. It was expressed in the efforts of individuals and groups to trace the history of their families, to understand their folk heritage, their communities, and their institutions. It was expressed in the efforts to preserve artifacts from the past—lighthouses, bridges, buildings—each a living reminder of the state as it was. It was expressed in the massive volunteer community efforts to clean up the environment so as to bequeath a portion of the state's natural beauty to future generations.

These were not exercises in nostalgia. They were serious attempts to understand our present by understanding our past. Our Bicentennial efforts were only a beginning, however. Too often as a nation we go off on fashionable binges. I do not believe that we can afford to make history a passing Bicentennial fad.

Here in Minnesota we pride ourselves on our quality of life. As Harrison Salisbury has recently observed, there is a unique Minnesota Spirit. I firmly believe that much of this spirit comes from the living ties with the past that our state has cherished. We are not a bland, standardized people, living on the two-dimensional plane of the present, without depth or perspective. Nor are we a homogenized people, unaware of the widely varied cultures from which we have come. The sweat and sorrows and dreams of our grandparents and great-grandparents as they struggled to turn the prairies and forests of this tough, beautiful land of ours into farms and towns are still very close to most Minnesotans.

Even our political traditions of active citizen participation and maverick independence are with us each day—commemorated in the very names of our two major parties, the Independent Republicans[1] and the Democratic-Farmer-Labor parties.

Evidence that a strong sense of the past has taken firm root in all parts of the state is unmistakable. The impressive growth of county and local historical programs within the past generation proves this: recent expanded activities; collections of photographs, manuscripts, and museum items; marker programs; audio-visual presentations; sites and buildings protected from the onslaught of the bulldozers; lectures; county, township, and community histories are evidence of our people's hunger for knowledge of the past.

People of all ages have taken increasing interest in their neighborhoods, capturing the spirit of their communities in books, articles, films, and even in the physical renovation of the buildings that surround them. These activities received a powerful stimulus from the observance of the Minnesota Territorial Centennial in 1949 and was reinforced nine years later by the celebration of the Statehood Centennial. Also helping to create a favorable climate were two laws enacted by the State Legislature.

A 1953 Statute permitted county boards to make a special tax levy for the support of historical work, and in 1957 the Legislature enabled them to provide physical facilities and maintenance for historical societies. A study issued by the American Association for State and Local History shows that preservation of history has received its widest and most sympathetic support from local government in the Middle West, and that Minnesota leads the fifty states in the amount of public funds granted for historical purposes by boards of county commissioners.

Our own State Historical Society's surveys show that annual county support for history in Minnesota approximates a million dollars and that more than half of the State's eighty-seven counties are granting such support on a regular basis. Paralleling the steady growth of county organizations during the past decade have been two other significant trends. Regional organizations bringing counties and an occasional local group together have taken on an important role [and] another movement has gained momentum—the formation of local historical organizations and

---

1. [The Independent Republican name was adopted in 1975 to distance Republican Minnesotans from the Watergate scandal. The "Independent" tag was dropped in 1995.—J.W.]

ethnic historical groups. All of these draw on the skills offered by our state's historians and folklorists.

Ultimately, however, the values and uses of history and tradition must not be judged by the number of organizations and buildings, by the size of commemorations and displays, or by the quantity of money spent. Rather, they will be determined by the individuals who accept or reject the past as a meaningful and vital force in their lives.

The relevance of history to today's world has been widely questioned. Some argue that the traditional interpretation of American history is, in fact, only the history of the dominant ethnic group—or a glorification of the lucky winners in a vast free-for-all of exploitation that we have traditionally looked upon as building civilization in a wilderness.

In meeting the challenges posed by a new generation of relentlessly honest young people, we must be prepared to look at the past through fresh eyes. We may be startled at some of the insights that appear if for a moment we reverse our field of vision and look at the story of a town, county or region through the eyes of its vanquished.

We may see Indians driven from their homes and told by a chorus of well-meaning voices that nowhere in the future is there a place for their holy beliefs and cherished customs—that to survive they must deny their identity and become white men. We may see immigrants, torn between hope for the new world and homesickness for the old, watching their children slowly weaned from the old ways and the old language to become foreigners under their very roofs. We will see towns dead or dying along with the hopes that built them when the railroad located elsewhere. We will see farmers driven under by drought or debt or grasshoppers, packing up their few belongings and sadly moving on. We will see game destroyed, forests leveled, hillsides eroded, and streams polluted by careless greed.

And inevitably the question will arise: What have we now, and is it worth the cost? For some the answer may be yes, for others, no—but if history is to have meaning for the present and future, the questions must be honestly faced.

Preservation of our historic environment should be one of our major objectives. We must be sure that the bulldozer does not serve as a substitute for historic planning and preservation in the guise of progress. . . .

History is a humanized force in our increasingly impersonal and technological world. A sense of history can anchor us firmly in our own identity which will enable us better to understand our neighbors in the State, the Nation, and the world. My work as chairman of the Minnesota Bicentennial Commission gave me a heightened appreciation for the importance of history.

Since 1849, when the first Territorial Legislature chartered the Minnesota Historical Society, our state has been one with a strong sense of respect for its past. It is imperative that we continue and expand this tradition to preserve and interpret our history. This is especially true now when changes in our customs, our ways of life, and even in the environment around us are so rapid that they create great gaps of understanding between generations.

A community without a knowledge of its past is like a person with amnesia. It can exist and function from day to day, but its lack of memory leaves it without a feeling of purpose, direction, or identity. A sense of history is recognizing the influence of the past in the very web of our daily lives—in our habits of thought and speech, in the streets we walk through, in the ways we earn a living. It is in the touch of humility that comes with knowing that wherever we are in life, we stand upon the shoulders of those who have gone before. For, as I have said, history is all of us.

AFTERWORD
What He Didn't Tell Me

Jay Weiner

By his own assessment, Hy Berman was "the most disorganized person in the world" and, believe me, that's entirely possible. On top of that, by the time we started working together in 2015, a little bit of forgetfulness at age ninety might have kicked in.

Hy repeatedly told me he'd never kept any of his papers or personal documents. And the "Hy Berman Papers" at the University of Minnesota Archives were, indeed, odd and spotty. They included clippings from nineteenth-century workers' and union newspapers. There were perhaps two thousand index cards with notes from primary sources. I found haphazard correspondence about the University's Department of History, including routine evaluations of faculty members, and an ad hoc collection of internal memos about filling out University forms and reappointments of colleagues.

And letters detailing missed deadlines for expected articles.

"I badly need to know when we may expect your article on Edward McGrady," wrote Sarah Ferrell, managing editor of the *Dictionary of American Biography* in November 1975. As far as I can tell, Hy never wrote the article.

So I figured that, in the wake of Hy's death, as I prepared this book I would have my interviews, others' interviews, and the wonderful collection of videos in Hy's past to work with, and I'd try my best to complete this project without him. But after he died, his family cleaned out his and Betty's house on Seabury Avenue in Minneapolis and what should be discovered but *twenty-two boxes* of pretty random stuff . . . lots of stuff. Letters, original drafts of articles, news clippings, notes from his college and graduate school years, job prospects, photographs, high school report cards. Lots of stuff.

File folders labeled "Columbia—Nevins Notes" and "India—1964," which are what they sound like. Letters written to him by his father in Yiddish. A few letters from angry students who received low grades or from happy students describing how he changed their lives. I painstakingly shoveled my way through those boxes and learned a lot.

I learned that in telling me his stories, Hy didn't volunteer much about some remarkable events. Was it disorganization? Forgetfulness? Or intent? In retrospect, we spent a relatively short period of time together. I'm thinking that had we worked for a year and had my own reporting uncovered material, he would have said, "Oh, right, I forgot about that!" And we would have dived deeper. His death erased those opportunities.

Three episodes stand out.

One is his somber and dramatic lecture about the Jewish Anti-Fascist Committee in which he finally, publicly, and painfully denounced his Communist past. He had quietly split from the Communist Party in 1952 with his review in *Historia Judaica* of Solomon Schwarz's book *The Jews in the Soviet Union*. But he had never made a full public denunciation of communism or the party. In our interviews, Hy had offhandedly mentioned a lecture he had given in more recent years but didn't elaborate or suggest its importance.

As I went through our interview transcripts, I wondered about this lecture, and I began asking around. His speech about the doomed leaders of the Anti-Fascist Committee was given on November 10, 2002, at the Sabes Jewish Community Center in St. Louis Park, Minnesota, to a group called the Yiddish *Vinkl*, which is, mostly, elderly Jews who are seeking to preserve the Yiddish language and Yiddish culture. Neal Gosman, who has been active in the group, tracked down the video for me. What's so powerful about Hy's remarks is just how remorseful, and almost timid, he appears. It's an emotional presentation fifty years after he says he split from the Party.

In it, as if tolling a bell for the victims, he details the lives and deaths of the thirteen members of the Anti-Fascist Committee who were tried, convicted, and executed by the Stalin regime. "Let me read their names, who they are, and when they were arrested," he says, solemnly. "We all know when they died."

You can see in him the remnants of reluctance and the sadness of resignation that, in retrospect, he was wrong in believing in what he believed and misguided in supporting what he supported.

"Now, what was their crime? Their crime was being Yiddish, speaking Yiddish, perpetuating Yiddish, having a sense of peoplehood with the Jewish people, which, of course, for some of them was a new reawakening, particularly after [World War II] when the results of the war were known."

But it is his self-criticism and that of his parents that's particularly jarring as he concluded that lecture when he is seventy-seven years old.

"Let me end this discussion by saying that I was one of those who believed firmly in the future of socialism as practiced in the Soviet Union. I was one of those who strongly believed that the Soviet Union was allowing for wide dissemination of Yiddish cultural activities. I was wrong, terribly wrong. As a matter of fact, so wrong that I now regret my early upbringing, my parents' devotion, and my faith in that system."

Throughout the Jack Stuart interviews and mine, Hy spoke so fondly of his early days in that leftist milieu. Sure, he discussed with me his understanding that his Communist connections were, as he said, an attraction to a "false god," but he never directed me to this deep self-criticism. There was real distress in those 2002 words that I never saw or heard in our interviews thirteen years later.

Another episode that is especially enigmatic was his testimony at the 1998 Minnesota tobacco trial, the legally named *State of Minnesota et al. v. Philip Morris et al.* The state of Minnesota and Blue Cross and Blue Shield of Minnesota sued a collection of tobacco companies and tobacco industry organizations for conspiring to defraud American smokers about the health harms of cigarettes. Hy, always the defender of and advocate for the little guy, did something really weird. He testified for the defense.

That is, he was a witness *for* the tobacco companies *against* the state. That baffled the local lawyers working for the state and startled the news media.

Unfortunately, I never got a chance to ask him about it. He didn't volunteer it, and frankly—though I guess I should have been—I wasn't aware of it during the months we regularly met; I found transcripts of his testimony in the treasure trove of boxes his family found in his house after his death.

As it turned out, over the forty years of litigation around tobacco, industry lawyers traditionally kicked off their cases with a local historian. The idea—after weeks of testimony from the plaintiffs—was to show that, heck, everybody knows that tobacco is harmful and so why blame the tobacco companies for the public health tragedy that is cigarette smoking? They all got lung cancer and died knowingly, or so the defense went.

Because Hy was the state's best-known and most respected public historian, the tobacco forces went with him as their expert. With the aid of some graduate students, Hy presented a narrative about the public knowledge of the hazards of cigarettes dating back to Christopher Columbus and on to the modern era of news media in Minnesota. And he said in his direct testimony to the tobacco lawyers that he and his students examined "hundreds of thousands" of news articles that documented the health dangers of cigarettes.

Hy could not help being his inimitable, charming self on the witness stand for a couple of days. When Peter Bleakley, the lead lawyer for the tobacco group, wanted Berman to repeat the volume of his research for the jury, Hy reiterated, yes, his research involved "hundreds of thousands" of articles. But he added, "Oh, I can't count them. I'd be very happy to take the jury to my study at home, a couple of minutes away from here, to take them up there and show them the boxes and boxes and boxes of material, the filing cabinets of material that we went through. My wife will even make some coffee, if you want."

But the tables were turned when the state's lead attorney, Michael Ciresi, confronted Hy the next day on cross-examination. Even before Hy took the stand, Ciresi and the state had challenged his expertise on the topic. After all, he was a labor historian, not a tobacco expert. Ciresi was able to find a huge hole in Hy's research. It had to do with a book written in 1968 by the University of Minnesota's own former Medical School dean Harold S. Diehl. Diehl was a vigilant antismoking advocate who, after leaving the University, became the head of research and medical affairs at the American Cancer Society.

It turned out that tobacco lawyer Bleakley had asked Berman about some of Diehl's writings but not about his 1968 book, which asserted that most Americans were not aware of the deep hazards of smoking. On this, Ciresi went in for the kill with Hy and to show the jurors that the tobacco folks were less than forthcoming. Berman acknowledged that he had read the book and had actually gotten it at the library in Diehl Hall—named after the very same dean and author at the University's Medical School. Diehl's book was published about five years after the first U.S. Surgeon General's Advisory Committee on Smoking and Health report.

Ciresi proceeded to show Hy the preface of Diehl's book in which Diehl wrote, "Surveys indicate that most people have heard of a relationship between cigarette smoking and cancer but that many of them consider the risk small and remote. Most people know little or nothing about the heart disease, the chronic bursitis and emphysema, and the other illnesses that frequently result from smoking."

Then, the cross-examination ensued:

Ciresi: And this is a physician who dealt intimately with this issue at the time, correct?

Berman: That is correct.

Ciresi: He would be a better historian of that age than you would be, wouldn't he?

Berman: He's the living practitioner, let's put it that way.

Ciresi: He is the embodiment of the historian at that time, isn't he?

Berman: He was a participant observer, as we would call it.

Ciresi: And if you go on, sir, to the next page. Now even Dr. Diehl was surprised by the lack of knowledge of people, wasn't he? Wasn't he, sir?

Berman: Yes, and that's why he wrote this book.

Ciresi: And then if you go down a couple paragraphs, he talks about a major cause of that public skepticism, doesn't he?

Berman: He does.

Ciresi: And he says that a major cause of the public skepticism about the harmfulness of smoking has been the cleverness of advertising promoting the habit, correct?

Berman: That's what he says, yes, sir.

Ciresi: Says, "Another cause has been the misleading propaganda of the cigarette industry." Correct?

Berman: That's what he says, yes, sir.

And it went on and on. Even though he was the defendants' witness, Hy was basically agreeing with the guts of the plaintiff's case: that the tobacco companies purposely kept information from the public. To those who were in the courtroom, it even looked as if Hy was just waiting to flip to the state's side. As Elizabeth Stawicki of Minnesota Public Radio reported then, "It was hard to know who Berman testified for. When he stepped down from the witness stand, he gave a thumbs up and a warm handshake to the state's attorney Mike Ciresi."

Others, sitting in earshot of Ciresi and Berman, heard Hy say, "Mike, you just killed me." No matter, Hy had been an expert paid well by the tobacco lawyers, investing, he testified, 1,200 hours of research into the project. In the end, Hy would joke to others that the brick patio off the kitchen at the Seabury Avenue house was courtesy of the tobacco industry.

After his first day of testifying, there was a meeting in the chambers of Ramsey County judge Kenneth Fitzpatrick where two things were revealed. One was that Hy received "some threatening phone calls" because of his testimony for the tobacco industry. Among them, according to the transcript of the in-chambers session was, "Years ago you defended Commie pinkos and now you're defending tobacco companies. Don't you have any conscience?" Also, Fitzpatrick warned the tobacco lawyers that Berman shouldn't talk to jury members. "If he does that a second time, I will ban him from the courtroom," the judge said. Apparently, Hy just couldn't help himself from being his friendly, chatty self.

And then there are two family stories: his wife, Betty's, and the death of their seven-year-old daughter, Michelle, or Shelly.

There was only one ground rule Hy sought when he handed that blue three-ring binder to me and asked for help with this book. This wasn't to be about his family. It was to be about his work. But a few things slipped into our interviews.

I actually learned of Betty's time in Auschwitz inadvertently when the Bermans visited our home for dinner. Hy hadn't volunteered it during our earliest interviews. The revelation came during a conversation that turned to Israel. Hy wasn't a Zionist, but he had spent time in Israel and was, of course, a lover, promoter, and observer of Jewish culture and an expert on anti-Semitism. As our discussion turned to some criticism of Israel, Betty said something like, "I can't listen to that anymore, not since I got out of Auschwitz."

Well, if that's not an eyebrow raiser of a comment, nothing is, and it's a dinner conversation stopper, too. Soon after, at one of our interview sessions, I asked Hy about it, and he finally told me Betty's story—about her mother's death in the concentration camp's gas chamber, about Betty's forced slavery in Dresden, about her escape with an aunt, about their hiding by a sympathetic German family, and about her eventual immigration to the United States, most of which is detailed in Carole Bell Ford's book *After the Girls Club: How Teenaged Holocaust Survivors Built New Lives in America.*

Their daughter's death came suddenly in 1971. Hy and Betty had two other children by then, Ruth born in 1958 and Steve a year later. Ruth is a now a writer and editor in California, and Steve has a Ph.D. in plant biology from the University of Minnesota and lives in California too. Both were born while the Bermans still lived in New York. As I tried to get Hy to speak about his kids, he interrupted.

"Then a third one comes along in 1964 when we were here in Minnesota," he said. "But she passed away, a tragic loss, you know. An aneurism at the age of seven."

I tried to offer my condolences when he volunteered, "That was the heaviest personal psychological blow I've ever received in my life. It's very unusual for a child to die that way, but that's what happened. It was unexpected. Here in the house, yes." He explained that he was able to take a couple of months off, including a month in Arizona with Betty, Ruth, and Steve. And we never got a chance to talk of Shelly again.

I'm not sure what it means, but Shelly died on Sunday, November 28. Her father died on Sunday, November 29, forty-four years and one day apart.

Hy's death triggered news media obituaries, editorials, and a public outpouring of appreciation in online comments and Facebook postings rarely given to historians or academicians of any kind.

On December 3, 2015, the sanctuary at Temple Israel synagogue in Minneapolis was about two-thirds filled for his funeral. Hy was not a religious man, but the Bermans were longtime members of one of the nation's largest Reform Jewish congregations. Of course, stories were shared.

His great friend David Noble spoke from his wheelchair of meeting Hy sixty years earlier: "It was love at first sight." He reported on their early conversations about how focused American history scholarship was on upper- and middle-class white, Protestant, and male leaders and how most university history departments were dominated by the same demographic, including two overt anti-Semites at the University of Minnesota when Hy arrived in 1961.

Days later, David would tell me in an interview that in their final lunch conversation weeks before Hy's death, Hy was angry and disappointed that labor history was falling by the wayside among young historians.

Eric Eskola, the *Almanac* television show cohost, offered a loving eulogy and quoted from a letter to the editor of the *Star Tribune*. "It said simply, 'Without Hy Berman, Minnesota is a little less Minnesotan.'"

Jack Stuart, who conducted the extensive and immensely helpful interviews before me, called Hy "the Zero Mostel of historians," a reference to the actor who starred in Broadway's *Fiddler on the Roof*. The gathering in the synagogue laughed knowingly of the entertaining, roly-poly old man whose wisdom was elevated by humor.

Rabbi Marcia Zimmerman of Temple Israel said, "Hy Berman lived a life of nuance. . . . He loved the world of ideas. . . . There was a way that Hy Berman stood out from other academics, and that was bringing those ideas down to Earth for the rest of us. . . . He understood what it meant to bring real life to the academic world, and the academic world to real life."

In fact, as well known an academic figure as Hy Berman was in Minnesota, he didn't publish much in academic journals and, frankly, he didn't give a damn that he did. When he was published, it was often in esoteric journals, such as *European Contributions to American Studies*. His writing was very different from his popular analyses in the media. "Despite the ability of the movement to overcome the tensions between its Leninist assumptions and its frontier radical roots during major periods of its effective existence, it was incapable of surviving in a changing America chained as it was to the imperatives of slavish support to the radically changing policies of the Soviet Union," was one exhausting sentence he wrote in an article from 1989 titled "Communism and the Frontier Tradition."

As he said many times in our interviews, he was far more interested in translating history for his students, the news media, and popular audiences than writing articles for a handful of other Ph.D.s to (maybe) read. And when it came to his occasional op-eds in the Twin Cities newspapers, Hy's writing was crisp. He was truly a people's historian with limited time for the rules of academia.

Rules or not, he loved the University of Minnesota, which was proved by his devotion to faculty governance and curriculum development, and his belief that private philanthropy and sponsored research are critical to the success of the University's faculty and students.

I was surprised by a presentation he gave in 1988 to the President's Club, which is the group of high-end U donors. He actually flew back from Europe to make the presentation, and it was one I wouldn't have expected from an ardent public education advocate. He praised the role—the necessary role, in his mind—of private philanthropy in promoting the excellence and reputation of the University. He cited funding in the areas of science and technology, such as the development of taconite by Dr. E. W. Davis and the impact funding and that discovery had on the economy of Northeast Minnesota.

"But less well known has been the tremendous achievements made possible in the areas of the arts, social policy, and international understanding," he told the donors. "Some would argue that the payoff for technological and industrial research can be, and often is, self-serving for those individuals and corporations that fund such research. . . . No one can, however, argue that contributions to the arts or to social policy research have a self-serving motivation."

He pointed to the policy creation of farm subsidies by University agronomists, and the policy work of Minnesota and University of Wisconsin economists in the development of the Social Security system in the 1930s. He credited private funding of University cultural programs in attracting the likes of Sir Tyrone Guthrie when he wanted a regional theater somewhere in the United States. "In the arts and the humanities, in public policy areas central to the well-being of the body politic, in the development of technological breakthroughs that enhance our economic health, and in the expansion and deepening of our role as an international university, the work of friends and supporters of the University has been crucial," he said.

Hy was, I guess, unpredictable. While softened by his twinkling eyes, his loose-fitting colorful sweaters, and his avuncular warmth, his ego was sizable. He loved his exposure on *Almanac*—with about ninety appearances, I was told—and cherished his regular connections with the local reporters. At Hy's funeral, Eskola related an encounter he had with Hy at the same ninetieth birthday party that triggered this book. "He motioned me over and with some annoyance said he hadn't been on *Almanac* in a year," Eskola said. "He said his body wasn't what it was"—Eskola pointed to his head—"'but I've still got it up here.' And he sure did."

Hy always wanted to share all the intersections of his life with all sorts of Hall of Famers, from the Communist Gus Hall to the historian John Hope Franklin to the perennial political candidate Harold Stassen to artist George Morrison. No doubt, Hy enjoyed being with the "in crowd," and he deserved to be.

As I watched years of older videos or listened to audio from the 1960s, '70s, and '80s, I saw an intense, serious professor and pundit. He was a scholar in full, soaring in his insight, bold in his confidence, and, most things considered, mostly accurate in his fact offering. He spoke in full sentences—periods and question marks clear in his discourse. He was a professor from central casting. His 1966 interview conducted by a young Garrison Keillor on KUOM and cited in chapter 3 is remarkable. Berman is encyclopedic in his understanding of Minnesota's history with regard to radical politics, and yet he'd been in the state for fewer than five years. In listening to the recording, I was also struck by the respect he showed during the hour's show for the twenty-three-year-old student interviewer, already an affected and know-it-all radio personality, en route to becoming a Minnesota icon—and then fallen icon—himself.

Even in 2002, at the age of seventy-seven, when he delivered his emotional report about the demise of the Jewish Anti-Fascist Committee, he was an extraordinary lecturer, using a minimal amount of notes, with a great sense of timing, passion, and even, for effect, hyperbole. He was, simply, an intellectual force even if, to those who only saw him on television or heard him on the radio, Hy was everyone's fun and intelligent uncle, someone to hug rather than someone to argue with.

And what I'm calling his ego was also his pride in having achieved so much and, sometimes, not receiving the recognition or respect he felt he deserved at the University, especially from his colleagues who thought him to be "too popular" to be taken seriously.

An example: In 1977, soon after Rudy Perpich became governor, the capitol reporter for the *Minneapolis Star*, Betty Wilson, wrote a glowing article about Berman's influence on Perpich and his policies. In one of the boxes that Hy's family discovered in his and Betty's house was a trove of material he must have retrieved from his parents after their deaths. Among those papers was a copy of the Wilson article with a handwritten 3 x 5 card attached:

Dear Ma,
This is an article about me and the new Governor—I hope you like it—
Love—Hy

Berman was fifty-one years old when he wrote the card.

Nearly four decades later, Hy was still thinking of his parents, of his upbringing, and his left-wing political DNA. One night in 2014 at Tom SenGupta's Schneider Drug pharmacy (and for some reason I videotaped this before I knew I'd even be working with him on this book), Hy stood. His cane was firmly in his right hand supporting him, his left hand moved with commitment and New York Jewishness as he spoke, and he explained why the working class—"the common person"— needed a monument in the Twin Cities. It was around this concept of a monument that I first got to know Hy over martinis and dinner.

The audience that night had an average age of seventy and numbered twenty-five at most, but one could imagine a lecture hall of three hundred youngsters in the palm of Professor Berman's hand.

"I am the son of immigrants who arrived in this country impoverished, and my parents—from the left wing side of politics—never quite felt part of this society, but always wanted to fit in," he said. "In my view, they were ordinary people who did extraordinary things. It is my belief that we should commemorate and honor those ordinary folks who opposed tyranny and oppression and stood for justice and what is right. From their experience we can learn how we ourselves can have an impact on society, and change the norm of society."

On the afternoon of December 3, 2015, a handful of cars followed the hearse that carried the body of Hy Berman through the streets of South Minneapolis to the Temple Israel Memorial Park Cemetery. The cantor sang, the rabbi quickly uttered prayers, and the graveside service was brief and chilly. The workers turned the pulleys to slowly lower the tiny and simple pine box to the resting place of Minnesota's most memorable history teacher.

ACKNOWLEDGMENTS

This book would not have been possible without the encouragement—nay, the insistence—of Hy's wife, Betty, and the support of his children, Steve and Ruth.

Many thanks to Jack Stuart for graciously sharing the transcripts of his interviews with Hy and me, thereby providing the critical core to this book.

Thanks to Max Edwards, Eric Eskola, Jessica Farrell, Neal Gosman, Eric Kaler, Al Levine, Al Milgrom, Erik Moore, David Noble, Amy Phenix, Tom SenGupta, Julie Slapp, Al Stern, Lori Sturdevant, Temple Israel, and various librarians of the University of Minnesota Libraries and Archives.

Thank you to Erik Anderson, Doug Armato, Kristian Tvedten, and Laura Westlund of the University of Minnesota Press for their guidance, patience, and support, and to Mary Byers for her meticulous and helpful copyediting.

As always, loving thanks to Ann Juergens for everything.

All the documents I sorted through to support and confirm Hy's words and my understanding of him are, thanks to the Berman family, now housed in the University of Minnesota's Archives.

Jay Weiner
St. Paul, Minnesota

INDEX

Black Power movement, 54, 55–56
Bleakley, Peter, 156, 157
Blegen, Theodore, 42
Board of Foreign Scholarships, 93
Bookbinder, Hy, 85
Booth, Cameron, xiii
Borchert, John, 58
Bradley, Omar, 19
Brezhnev, Leonid, 96, 115
Brodbeck, May, 83
Brody, William, 133
Brooklyn College (Brooklyn, N.Y.), 39,
43–44, 137
Brooks, Ronnie, 111
Bruininks, Bob, 131
Bund, the, 3
Bush, George W., 117, 126

Cahan, Abe, 32
Camejo, Peter, 55
Camp Kinderland (Brooklyn, N.Y.),
10, 13, 14, 15, 16, 39; HUAC's in-
vestigation of, 17, 34, 35–37
Camp Swift (Austin, Tex.), 19
Camp Wo-Chi-Ca (Workers'
Children's Camp, N.Y.), 14–15
capitalism, 142, 143
Carlson, Arne, 122
Carman, Harry, 38–39, 41, 47
Carter, Jimmy, 107, 115
Center for Victims of Torture
(St. Paul, Minn.), 123
Chagall, Marc, 16
Chambers, Clarke A., xv, 49
Channel 2 (Twin Cities Public
Television): teaching a public his-
tory course on, 26, 137–40. See
also Almanac
Chase, Hal, 130
Chase, Ray P., 75–76, 77

Chase, Roe, 75
China: Communist Party in, 96, 97;
lecture tours in, 4, 89, 93–98, 105,
120, 142–43; Rudy Perpich's visit
to, 120
Christenson, Jerry, 134
Ciresi, Michael, 156–58
Citizens Alliance, 72
City College of New York, 10, 55;
purge of leftist faculty from, 12, 27;
teaching assistantship at, 26–27,
34; undergraduate degree from,
11–12, 24–26, 38
Civil Rights Act of 1964, 81
Clough, Shepard, 37–38
Coleman, Nick, 107
Coleman, Norm, 64
Columbia College of New York, 26,
34, 35, 37, 38–42
Commager, Henry Steele, 38, 42
Common Ground (journal), 69. See
also McWilliams, Carey
common man, monument to honor,
xii–xiii, 163
Communist Party, 17, 23; activities at
city universities, 11, 12; American
Student Union affiliated with, 10,
15; break from, 29–30, 32–35, 89,
105, 154; in China, 96, 97; first
contact with, 4–5; Henry Wallace
campaign run by, 31–32; involvement in Yiddish schools and
camps, 12–17, 91. See also American Communist Party; Leninism;
Marxism/Marxists; New Left student activism; socialism/Socialists
Coney Island (Brooklyn, N.Y.), 2–3
Cooperman, David "Dan," 52
Copland, Aaron, 16
culture: differences in, 16, 143;

immigrant, 127; Jewish, 12, 159; in Minneapolis and St. Paul, Minn., 46; at University of Minnesota, 133; Yiddish, 13, 29. *See also* internationalism; pluralism, cultural; theater; Yiddish language

University of Minnesota (Minneapolis, Minn.), 13, 55, 84, 161; African and African American Studies Department, 58–62; anti-Semitism at, 47, 130, 160; culture of, 133; economic crises at, 128, 131; emphasis on credentialing, 143–44; faculty union organizing efforts, 128–29, 132; first impression of, 1–2; Humphrey joins faculty, 83–86; Hy Berman Papers, 153; Immigration History Research Center, 49, 58; Iron Range research project, 49–52, 64–65, 127; new archives building, 112–13; presidents of, 127–36; retirement from, 136, 144–45; role in Chinese higher education, 94–95; Social Sciences program, 46, 48, 52, 56–58, 62, 132; teaching position, 45–48; tenure wars, 132–34

University of Minnesota Federation of Teachers, 128–29

Vecoli, Rudy, 49
Ventura, Jesse, 139, 140
Vietnam War: Humphrey changes position on, 83; Hy's opposition to, 53, 65–67, 81; Perpich's opposition to, 110–11
Voting Rights Act of 1965, 81

Wahl, Rosalie, 116
Wallace, George, 82, 83

Wallace, Henry: in 1948 presidential race, 31–32
Wechkin, Stanley, 35
Wellstone, Paul, xii, 116–17
Whitney, Wheelock, 119
Wilson, O. Meredith, 49, 50, 59, 127–28
Winter War, 15. *See also* World War II
Wisan, Joseph, 25, 26
Wolf, John Baptist, 47
Workmen's Circle, 13
World Trade Center (St. Paul, Minn.), 123
World War II: Holocaust, 30, 31, 78, 90, 158–59; service in, 17–21; Soviet Union in, 11, 15

Yiddish language, 71, 72, 132, 155; schools and camps conducted in, 12–17; spoken in Berman home, 2, 8, 91. *See also* culture: Yiddish; theater: Yiddish
Young Communist League (YCL), 13, 15, 16, 17
Young Pioneers of America (YPA), 13, 16
Yudof, Judy, 134
Yudof, Mark, 127, 134–36, 144–45

Ziebarth, E. W. "Easy," 57
Zimmerman, Marcia, 160
Zionism/Zionists, 29, 90, 159, 161

For more than forty years, **HY BERMAN** (1925–2015) was one of the most popular professors at the University of Minnesota, where he taught in the History Department from 1961 until 2004. He was widely known for his appearances on Twin Cities Public Television's *Almanac,* which solidified his role as the state's leading public historian. A former colleague of Hubert Humphrey and adviser to Minnesota governor Rudy Perpich, he was a learned and avuncular pundit on all things historical and political.

JAY WEINER is the author of *Stadium Games: Fifty Years of Big League Greed and Bush League Boondoggles* and *This Is Not Florida: How Al Franken Won the Minnesota Senate Recount,* both published by the University of Minnesota Press.